NEW 2018

COMMON CORE MATH

GRADE 4

PART II: FREE RESPONSE

Visit **www.argoprep.com** to get
FREE access to our online platform.

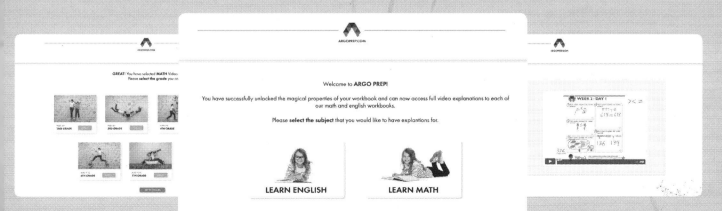

1000+ Minutes of Video Explanations and more!

Authors: Kellie Zimmer
Anayet Chowdhury
Eduard Suleyman
Vladislav Suleyman

Design: Vladislav Suleyman

At Argo Brothers, we are dedicated to providing quality and effective supplemental practice for your child. We would love to hear your honest feedback and **review** of our workbooks on **Amazon**.

Argo Brothers is one of the leading providers of supplemental educational products and services. We offer affordable and effective test prep solutions to educators, parents and students. Learning should be fun and easy! For that reason, most of our workbooks come with detailed video answer explanations taught by one of our fabulous instructors. Our goal is to make your life easier, so let us know how we can help you by e-mailing us at **info@argobrothers.com**.

OTHER BOOKS BY ARGO BROTHERS

Here are some other test prep workbooks by Argo Brothers you may be interested in. All of our workbooks come equipped with detailed video explanations to make your learning experience a breeze! Subscribe to our mailing list at www.argobrothers.com to receive custom updates about your education.

GRADE 2

GRADE 3

GRADE 4

GRADE 5

GRADE 6

GRADE 7

GRADE 4

GRADE 5

TABLE OF CONTENTS

HOW TO USE THE BOOK

This workbook is designed to give lots of practice with the math Common Core State Standards (CCSS). By practicing and mastering this entire workbook, your child will become very familiar and comfortable with the state math exam. If you are a teacher using this workbook for your student's, you will notice each question is labeled with the specific standard so you can easily assign your students problems in the workbook. This workbook takes the CCSS and divides them up among 20 weeks. By working on these problems on a daily basis, students will be able to (1) find any deficiencies in their understanding and/or practice of math and (2) have small successes each day that will build proficiency and confidence in their abilities.

You can find detailed video explanations to each problem in the book by visiting:
www.argoprep.com

We strongly recommend watching the videos as it will reinforce the fundamental concepts. Please note, scrap paper may be necessary while using this workbook so that the student has sufficient space to show their work.

For a detailed overview of the Common Core State Standards for 4th grade, please visit:
www.corestandards.org/Math/Content/4/introduction/

For more practice with 4th Grade Math, be sure to check out our other book
Common Core Math Workbook Grade 4: Multiple Choice

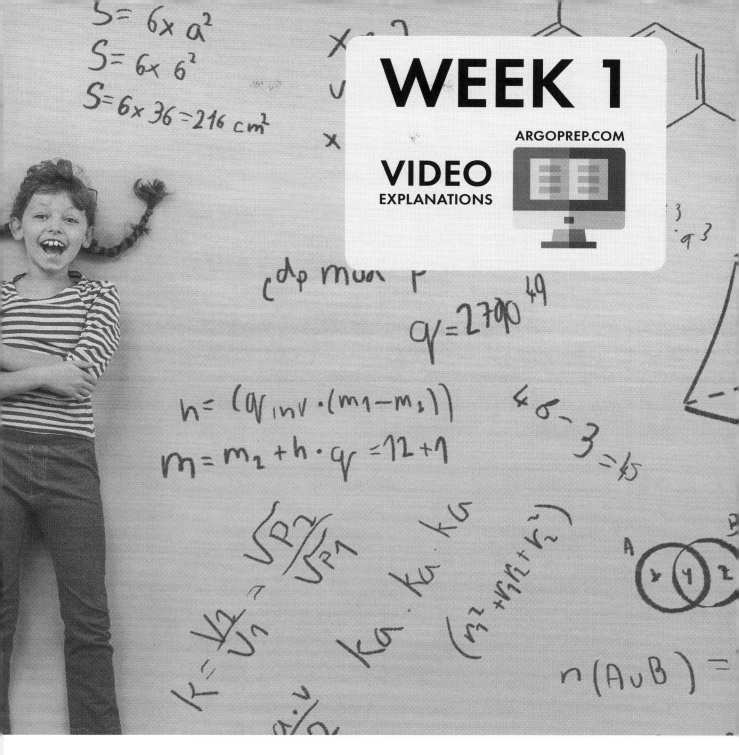

Week 1 is all about numbers – their names, their values and different ways of writing them. You'll also learn how to compare them using comparison symbols such as greater than (>), less than (<) and equal to (=).

You can find detailed video explanations to each problem in the book by visiting: ArgoPrep.com

1. Alec's dad runs 10 times as far as Alec. If Alec ran 7 miles last week, how far did his dad run?

4.NBT.1

2. Annie had $700 that was in $100 bills. How many $100 bills did Annie have?

4.NBT.1

3. There were 400 cookies for the fundraiser. If each box could hold 10 cookies, how many boxes would they need?

4.NBT.1

4. Betsy wrote a 3-digit number that was 10 times the number 50. What was her number?

4.NBT.1

5. Wilson walked 10 times as far as Roger ran. If Wilson walked 60 miles, how far did Roger run?

4.NBT.1

6. How many times larger is 8,000 than 80?

4.NBT.1

1. The main speaker spoke 10 times as long as the man who introduced him. The man who introduced the speaker spoke for 3 minutes. How long did the main speaker speak?

4.NBT.1

2. Harvey was 40 years old, which was 10 times the age of his son. How old is Harvey's son?

4.NBT.1

3. Jeanne went to the mall and bought 80 gumdrops, which was 10 times the number that Teresa bought. How many gumdrops did Teresa buy?

4.NBT.1

4. William had 20 bills for a total of $200. How much was each bill worth? (Every bill was the same denomination.)

4.NBT.1

5. How many times greater is 600 than 60?

4.NBT.1

6. The flagpole was 10 times as tall as the lamppost. If the lamppost was 10 meters, how tall was the flagpole?

4.NBT.1

1. What is 8,000 + 200 + 40,000 + 6 + 10 in standard form?

4.NBT.2

2. Write 16,412 in words.

4.NBT.2

3. Make a true number sentence using an inequality symbol and the numbers 57,819 and 58,016.

4.NBT.2

4. What is five hundred eighty-nine thousand, two when written in standard form?

4.NBT.2

5. Write a true number sentence using an inequality symbol and the numbers 14,982 and 41,237.

4.NBT.2

6. Write a 3-digit number that has a 4 that is 10 times the value of the 4 in 843.

4.NBT.1

1. Make a true number sentence using an inequality symbol and the numbers 12,457 and 12,398.

4.NBT.2

2. What is six hundred eight thousand, five hundred seventy-one when written in standard form?

4.NBT.2

3. What is 100,000 + 400 + 3 + 5,000 + 70,000 in standard form?

4.NBT.2

4. Write 125,081 in words.

4.NBT.2

5. Write 6 tens + 7 thousands + 3 ones + 8 hundreds in standard form.

4.NBT.2

6. Make a true number sentence using the numbers 700,000 + 50,000 + 2 + 10 and 750,012.

4.NBT.2

1. The hardware store had 10 times as many nails as Corbin. If Corbin had 2000 nails, how many nails did the hardware store have?

4.NBT.1

2. Write 254,092 in words.

4.NBT.2

3. What is 20,000 + 400 + 5 + 30 + 7,000 in standard form?

4.NBT.2

4. The farm was 10 times as large as McMillen Park. If the farm was 3,000 acres, how big was the park?

4.NBT.1

5. Write a true number sentence using the numbers 6,000 + 40 + 5 and 6,405.

4.NBT.2

6. Cassie only had $10 bills. If she had $500, how many $10 bills did she have?

4.NBT.1

 **DAY 6**
CHALLENGE
QUESTION
Using the numbers 5, 7, 0, 9 and 4, make a 5-digit number that has the largest possible value using those numbers once each.

4.NBT.2

This week we are going to practice rounding numbers. Rounding is useful when you don't need an exact number, but you need a rough estimate. You'll have the opportunity to add and subtract lots of numbers.

You can find detailed video explanations to each problem in the book by visiting:
ArgoPrep.com

1. What is 1,693 rounded to the nearest ten and hundred?

4.NBT.3

2. Round 13,697,054 to the tens and ten thousands places. Write a number sentence using those 2 rounded numbers and a comparison symbol.

4.NBT.3

3. What is 15,492 rounded to the nearest thousand?

4.NBT.3

4. What is 67,999 rounded to the nearest ten?

4.NBT.3

5. Round 349,760 to the hundreds and ten thousands places. Write a number sentence using those 2 rounded numbers and a comparison symbol.

4.NBT.3

6. Round 6,995 to the nearest ten.

4.NBT.3

WEEK 2 · DAY 2

---

1. What is 76,045,119 rounded to the nearest million and ten thousand?

4.NBT.3

---

2. What is 79,081,425 rounded to the nearest hundred thousand?

4.NBT.3

---

3. The number 672 could be rounded to 700 or 670, how is this possible?

4.NBT.3

---

4. Round 981,655 to the nearest hundred and the nearest ten thousand.

4.NBT.3

---

5. Round 8,799,999 to the nearest hundred. What is that number?

4.NBT.3

---

6. What is the smallest number that could round to 200 if we round to the nearest hundred?

4.NBT.3

1. If Ryan bought 144 apples, gave away 93 then bought 276 more, how many apples does he have now?

4.NBT.4

2. A record of Kim's bank account is shown below. She started with $5670 in her account.

Deposits (put money in account)	Withdrawals (took money out of account)
$1243	$500
$789	$396

How much money is in Kim's account now?

4.NBT.4

3. Round 8,721 and 4,386 to the nearest thousands then find the difference between the rounded numbers. Show your work.

4.NBT.3
4.NBT.4

4. Write a number sentence using these 3 numbers:

4,671   3,640   1,031

4.NBT.4

5. Find the sum of 210 + 7,819 + 76.

4.NBT.4

1. Round 2,598 and 3,849 to the nearest hundreds then add the rounded numbers. Show your work.

4.NBT.3
4.NBT.4

2. The grocery store had 5,000 apples on Monday morning. In the evening there were only 397 apples left. How many apples were bought on Monday?

4.NBT.4

3. The library had 7,852 books. Mary donated 509 books and the library had to discard 46 books that were in bad shape. How many books are in the library now?

4.NBT.4

4. What is the difference between 1,340 and 955?

4.NBT.4

5. The guests that visited the fair are shown below.

Day	Guests
Friday	2,809
Saturday	3,726
Sunday	1,954

How many guests attended either Saturday or Sunday?

How many more guests were there on the weekend than on Friday?

4.NBT.4

1. Find a number that would round to 8,100.

4.NBT.3

2. Round 7,891 and 4,528 to the nearest ten and then find the difference of the rounded numbers. Show your work.

4.NBT.3
4.NBT.4

3. Round 8,528,952 to the nearest million and nearest hundred.

4.NBT.3

4. Priscilla charged $3,198 at the electronics store. She then received a credit for a return on a TV for $1,407. Finally she bought a phone for $679. What should her credit card statement say she owes to the electronics store? Show your work.

4.NBT.4

5. What is 712 + 8,906 - 5,003?

4.NBT.4

6. Round 5,649 and 5,757 to the nearest hundred. Write a true number statement using the rounded numbers and a comparison symbol.

4.NBT.2
4.NBT.3

DAY 6
CHALLENGE QUESTION

What is the largest number that would round to 7,900 assuming you round to the nearest thousands place?

4.NBT.3

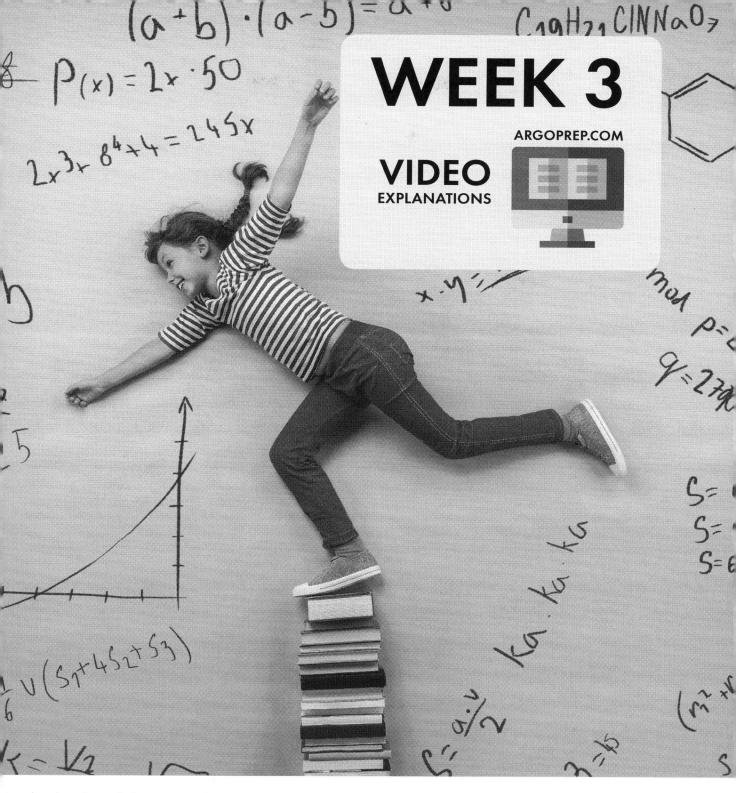

Week 3 has lots of division problems. Sometimes numbers go into other numbers "evenly" and sometimes there are remainders (or leftovers). Week 3 will provide lots of practice using division.

You can find detailed video explanations to each problem in the book by visiting:
ArgoPrep.com

Use the chart below to answer questions 1–3. The chart shows how many people rode on certain rides at the fair.

Ride	People
Tilt-A-Whirl	1,682
Matterhorn	914
Bumper Cars	798

1. Four times the number of people who rode Bumper Cars bought food. How many people bought food?

4.NBT.5

2. Two times as many people rode the Matterhorn the following day. How many people rode the Matterhorn the next day?

4.NBT.5

3. How many more people rode the Tilt-A-Whirl than the Matterhorn?

4.NBT.4

4. There were 15 rides at the fair that had 22 seats each. There were another 8 rides that could hold 31 people at one time.

   A. How many people could ride at one time on the 22-seater rides?
   B. How many people could ride at one time on the 31-seaters?
   C. If these were the only rides, how many people could ride at one time?
   D. If the 22-seater rides were tripled, how many people would they then be able to hold?

4.NBT.4

WEEK 3 · DAY 2

Use the chart below to answer questions 1–5. Jarrett Cars has lots all over the country. Some of the cars are shown below.

Car Color	Number of Cars
Green	1,268
Blue	4,573

1. Jarrett Cars had 5 times as many black cars as there were green cars. How many black cars were there?

4.NBT.5

2. There were 4 times as many silver cars as there were blue cars. How many silver cars were there?

4.NBT.5

3. If the number of green cars were rounded to the nearest thousand, then how many black cars would there be?

4.NBT.3
4.NBT.5

4. If the number of blue cars were rounded to the nearest hundred, then how many silver cars would there be?

4.NBT.3
4.NBT.5

5. The number of white cars is 2 times the total of the green and blue cars. How many white cars does Jarrett Cars have?

4.NBT.4
4.NBT.5

1. There are 3,000 bananas that will be shipped in bunches of 9 bananas each.

   A. How many bunches will there be?
   B. How many bananas will be leftover?

   4.NBT.6

2. There were 512 pairs of shoes to be packed into boxes. Each box can hold 6 pairs.

   A. How many boxes will be completely filled?
   B. Will there be any shoes left unpacked? If so, how many?

   4.NBT.6

3. Thomas can fit 8 chairs on the trailer and there are 301 chairs to be transported.

   A. How many trips will Thomas need to make?
   B. How many chairs will be transported on the last trip?

   4.NBT.6

Use the table below to answer questions 4–5.

Furniture	Number of Pieces
Chairs	2,890
Sofas	1,003

4. How many sofas and chairs were there in total?

   4.NBT.4

5. If there were 3 times as many loveseats as sofas, how many loveseats were there?

   4.NBT.5

1. There are boxes that can hold 6 cupcakes and boxes that can hold 8 cupcakes. There are 3,200 cupcakes. Which boxes would have the fewest leftover cupcakes? Show your work.

4.NBT.6

2. The banquet hall can seat 8 people at each table. There are 212 wedding guests.

   A. How many tables will be needed?
   B. How many people will be at the last table?

4.NBT.6

Use the chart below to answer questions 3–5. It shows the number of desserts at the wedding. Dessert trays can hold 5 desserts.

Chocolate cupcakes	102
Strawberry cheesecake	57
Vanilla ice cream	78

3. How many trays will be needed?

4.NBT.6

4. **A.** How many complete trays of cupcakes will there be?
   B. How many cupcakes will be on a tray with different desserts?

4.NBT.6

5. **A.** How many full trays will there be for the ice cream?
   B. How many full trays for the cheesecake?

4.NBT.6

1. There were 245 water bottles on each shelf at SuperStore. There are 9 shelves.

   A. How many water bottles are there?
   B. If the bottles were packed into bags that held 8 bottles each, how many bags would be needed?
   C. How many bottles would be in the last bag?

   4.NBT.5
   4.NBT.6

2. MegaStore has 5 times as many water bottles as Super Store. How many water bottles does MegaStore have?

   4.NBT.5

3. Round the number of bottles that MegaStore has to the nearest thousand.

   4.NBT.3

Use the table below to answer questions 4–5. It shows the amount of lemonade and tea that SuperStore has.

Drink	Gallons
Lemonade	984
Tea	472

4. If MegaStore has 6 times as much tea as SuperStore, how much tea does MegaStore have?

   4.NBT.5

5. If SuperStore evenly split their lemonade up among 3 different sections in the store, how many gallons of lemonade would each section have?

   4.NBT.6

DAY 6
CHALLENGE
QUESTION

Use the table to answer the questions.
Which would be more animals - 11 times Asheboro's mammals or 9 times Springfield's mammals?

If the zoos were to close and the reptiles were to be split up among 4 different zoos, how many reptiles would each zoo receive?

Animals	Springfield	Asheboro
Mammals	108	98
Reptiles	312	156

4.NBT.5/4.NBT.6

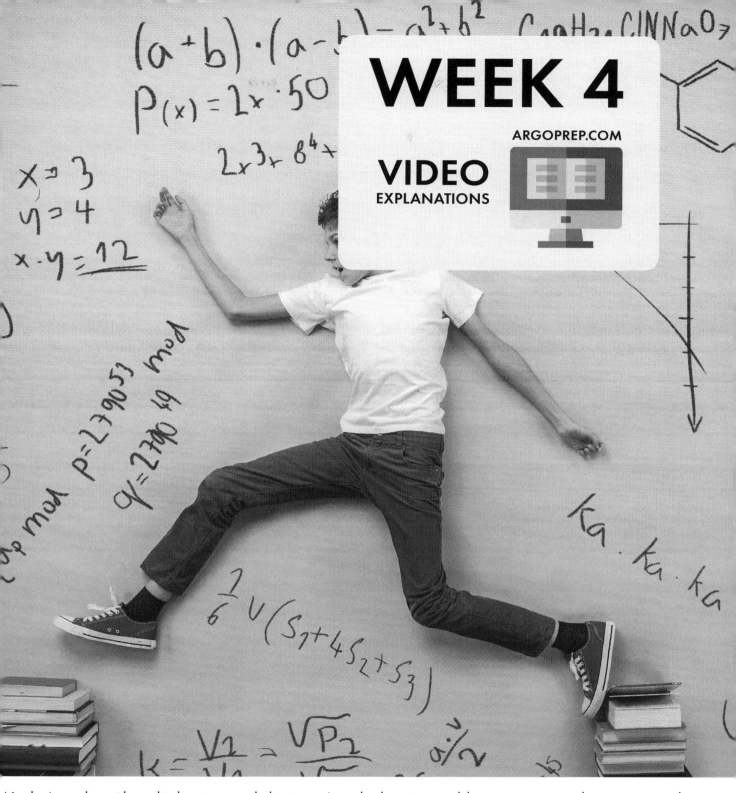

WEEK 4

ARGOPREP.COM

VIDEO EXPLANATIONS

Week 4 works with multiplication and division. A multiplication problem is just a number sentence that shows how much larger one number is than another. Key words like "product" or "times" means to multiply and key words like "quotient" means to divide.

You can find detailed video explanations to each problem in the book by visiting:
ArgoPrep.com

1. Write an equation that shows why 42 is 3 times as many as 14.

4.OA.1

2. Use 36 as the number being compared.

    A. How many times greater is 36 than 9?
    B. How many times greater is 36 than 18?
    C. How many times greater is 36 than 6?

4.OA.1

Use the chart below to answer questions 3–4.

Building	Height
Goody Arena	312
Willis Place	208
Nexus Tower	104

3. How many times taller is Goody Arena than Nexus Tower?

4.OA.1

4. How many times taller is Willis Place than Nexus Tower?

4.OA.1

5. Round 541,999 to the thousands and tens places. Then write a number sentence using those 2 rounded numbers and a comparison symbol.

4.OA.1

1. Use the number 12 to write as many statements as possible about how many times larger 12 is than another number. The first one has been done for you.

The number 12 is 12 times larger than the number 1.

4.OA.1

2. Write an equation that shows why 28 is 4 times as many as 7.

4.OA.1

3. There are 260 parachutes that need to be split evenly among 9 planes.

   A. How many parachutes will each plane get?
   B. How many parachutes will be left behind?

4.NBT.6

4. Use the equation 5 × 6 = 30 to write 2 statements that compare the numbers in the equation.

4.OA.1

5. Stephanie is 32 years old, Johnny is 16 years old and Ralphie is 8 years old.

   A. How many times older is Stephanie than Ralphie?
   B. How many times older is Stephanie than Johnny?

4.OA.2

6. Write an equation that shows why 72 is 8 times as many as 9.

4.OA.1

1. Draw a model for the equation: $5 \times 4 = 20$ that shows that 20 is 4 times larger than 5.

   4.OA.1

2. The play was on Thursday and Friday nights. Three times as many people attended on Friday night as attended Thursday. There were 126 people that attended on Thursday.

   A. How many people attended on Friday night?
   B. How many people attended on both nights combined?

   4.OA.2

3. The gymnastics team won 5 times as many medals as the basketball team. The gymnastics team won 30 medals.

   A. How many medals did the basketball team win?
   B. How many medals did the 2 teams win altogether?

   4.OA.2

4. Three people ran or walked in a park. Their distances are shown below.

Runner/Walker	Distance
Addie	18 mi
Morgan	3 mi
Aiden	6 mi

   A. How many times farther did Addie walk than Aiden?
   B. How many times farther did Aiden walk than Morgan?

   4.OA.2

5. Last week Jeff watched 7 times as much TV as Jenna. Jenna watched 7 hours.

   A. How many hours of TV did Jeff watch?
   B. How many hours did Jeff and Jenna watch altogether?

   4.OA.2

1. It is twice as far from Atlanta to Jacksonville as it is from Atlanta to Charlotte. If it is a 4 hour drive from Atlanta to Charlotte, how long would it take to drive from Atlanta to Jacksonville?

4.OA.2

2. Jerry's project took him 8 days to complete. Sabrina took 3 times as long on her project.

   A. How long did Sabrina's project take?
   B. How long did Jerry and Sabrina spend on their projects together?

4.OA.2

3. What equation could describe the model below?

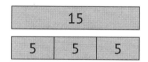

4.OA.1

4. Maci trained 6 times longer than Kasey. Maci trained for 12 weeks.

   A. How long did Kasey train?
   B. How long did Maci and Kasey train altogether?

4.OA.2

5. The movie was 4 times longer than the cartoon. The cartoon was 32 minutes long.

   A. How long was the movie?
   B. How long was the movie and the cartoon combined?

4.OA.2

The chart below shows the distance from a city in Texas to 3 other cities. Use it to answer questions 1-2

City	Distance (mi)
Dallas	1,235
Houston	517
San Antonio	384

1. There is a city in Texas and its distance from 3 other Texas cities is shown above.

   A. If Mayville is 3 times as far as Dallas, how many miles away is Mayville?
   B. If San Antonio is 4 times as far as Skoggins, how many miles away is Skoggins?   4.OA.2

2. What is the difference in the distances of Dallas and Houston?

   4.NBT.4

3. Mark spent 5 times as much money as Lori. Lori spent $65.

   A. How much money did Mark spend?
   B. How much did Mark and Lori spend altogether?   4.OA.2

4. The new road was 4 times shorter than the old road. The old road was 20 kilometers. How many kilometers is the new road?

   4.OA.2

5. Tobey grew 2 times as much than Maggie. Maggie grew 8 inches.

   A. How much did Tobey grow?
   B. How much did Tobey and Maggie grow altogether?   4.OA.2

DAY 6
CHALLENGE QUESTION

Marty had 3 times as many points as Gena. Gena had 5 times as many points as Paul. If Gena had 10 points how many points did Marty and Paul have?

4.OA.2

WEEK 5

ARGOPREP.COM

VIDEO EXPLANATIONS

This week allows you to exercise what you practiced last week by solving multi-step word problems. You'll work with factors to find numbers that go into other numbers evenly. You will also be asked to find factor pairs.

You can find detailed video explanations to each problem in the book by visiting:
ArgoPrep.com

Use the chart below to answer questions 1–3. The chart shows the color and number of bikes that Bike-A-Rama had at their store.

Bike color	Number
Blue	4,802
Pink	1,975
Black	3,160

1. How many bikes did Bike-A-Rama have at their store?

4.OA.3

2. The store can fit 7 bikes into one box for shipping, how many full boxes would there be?

4.OA.3

3. How many bikes would not be shipped?

4.OA.3

4. Write a number sentence using the standard form for 4 tens + 3 thousands + 6 hundreds and three thousand, six hundred four using a comparison symbol.

4.NBT.2

5. The football team sold 596 buckets of laundry detergent as a fundraiser. Each bucket sold earned $8.

   A. Write an equation to find out how much money, M, the team earned.
   B. How much money did the football team make?

4.OA.3

1. Carly had to unpack 62 boxes that contained 25 cushions in each box. Then she had to repack them into boxes that held 4 cushions each.

   A. How many cushions were there?
   B. How many full boxes would Carly have?
   C. How many cushions would be unboxed?

4.OA.3

2. For the picnic, they barbequed 4,012 hamburgers and 3,950 hot dogs.

   A. How many burgers and dogs were grilled?
   B. If each person ate 2 items (either a burger or dog), how many people could eat?
   C. How many burgers and dogs would be left?

4.OA.3

3. Veggie Patch restaurant served 98 orders of stuffed peppers. Each order had 4 peppers, 3 tomatoes, 1 onion and 4 carrots. How many vegetables were used in the 98 orders?

4.OA.3

4. Round 7,891 to the tens and to the hundreds. Write a number sentence using the 2 rounded numbers using a comparison symbol.

4.NBT.3

5. The 6 roommates split their bills evenly. They are shown below.

Rent	$2350
Electricity	$316
Cable/Phone	$298

   A. Write an equation that can be used to find out how much each roommate owes. Let *R* stand for one roommate's expenses.
   B. How much will each roommate have to pay?

4.OA.3

1. Using only 2 and 5 as factors, what are the first 5 multiples of 2 and 5?

4.OA.4

2. Which number has more factors 18 or 24? Show your work.

4.OA.4

3. Using only 3 and 8 as factors, what are the first 4 multiples of 3 and 8?

4.OA.4

4. Which number has more factors 12 or 15? Show your work.

4.OA.4

5. When Camryn graduated from college, she received 5 gifts of $50, 2 gifts of $415, and 1 gift of $2600. Then she bought a bed for $710 and a refrigerator for $1298. How much of the gift money remained?

4.NBT.4

6. Numbers that have 2 and 3 as factors also have 6 as a factor. Why is that?

4.OA.4

1. Using only 3 and 6 as factors, what are the first 5 multiples of 3 and 6?

4.OA.4

2. Which number has more factors – 32 or 36? Show your work.

4.OA.4

3. Numbers that have 9 as a factor also have 3 as a factor. Why is that?

4.OA.4

4. Kara had 24 belts that could be packaged any way she liked as long as (1) there were at least 2 packages, (2) all the packages had the same number of belts and (3) there were no belts leftover. What are all the possibilities of how many belts could be in the packages?

4.OA.4

5. Cooper Farms has 9,860 eggs that need to be placed into cartons that can hold 6 eggs. Only full cartons can be shipped.

    A. Write an equation that can be used to find C, the number of cartons needed.
    B. How many full cartons would there be?
    C. How many eggs would not be shipped?

4.NBT.6

6. Which number has more factors – 15 or 21? Show your work.

4.OA.4

1. Micah had 18 bottles of water that could be packaged any way he liked as long as (1) there were at least 2 packages, (2) all the packages had the same number of bottles and (3) there were no bottles leftover. What are all the possibilities of how many bottles could be in the packages?

4.OA.4

2. The distance Jaren hiked is shown below.

Monday	10 miles
Tuesday	8 miles
Wednesday	12 miles
Thursday	20 miles
Friday	5 miles

A. How many miles did Jaren hike?
B. If he hiked the same distance each day, how far would he have to hike each day to travel the same distance?

4.OA.3

3. Liam earns $9/hour when he works at the coffee shop and $15/hour when he bales hay. If he worked in the shop for 10 hours last week and baled hay for 21 hours, how much money did Liam earn? Show your work.

4.OA.3

4. Which number has the most factors – 10, 14 or 18? Show your work.

4.OA.4

5. Numbers that have 2 and 5 as factors also have 10 as a factor. Why is that?

4.OA.4

DAY 6
CHALLENGE
QUESTION

Sarah made $28 selling her shells. Each shell costs the same amount. She earned more than $1 per shell and she sold more than 1 shell. How many shells might she have sold and for what price? List all possibilities.

4.OA.4

Patterns and rules are covered in Week 6. You will be asked to find patterns or make patterns by following certain rules like "add 1" or "subtract 4". You'll also start working with fractions to find equivalent fractions and using models to show what fractions can look like.

You can find detailed video explanations to each problem in the book by visiting:
ArgoPrep.com

1. The rule is "add 5" and it starts with an even number. Write 4 numbers that fit this number pattern.

   4.OA.5

2. Ella liked the rule "add 3" and Emma preferred the rule "add 4" If Ella started at 12 and Emma started at 10, who would reach the number 30 first? Show your work.

   4.OA.5

3. A pattern starts with the number 50 and uses the rule "subtract 3". What are the first 4 numbers after 50?

   4.OA.5

4. Which number has more factor pairs 99 or 24? Show your work.

   4.OA.4

5. Draw a shape pattern that shows the rule "subtract 2".

   4.OA.5

6. What "rule" is used in the number pattern: 112, 102, 92, 82...?

   4.OA.5

1. Look at the pattern below.

   A. What "rule" is being used?

   B. What might the next shape look like?

4.OA.5

2. Sam used the rule "subtract 5" and started at 42. Tom used the rule "subtract 2" and began at 22. Who would reach the number 12 first? Show your work.

4.OA.5

3. A pattern starts with the number 23 and uses the rule "add 6". What are the first 4 numbers after 23?

4.OA.5

4. Write the 2 numbers below in standard form and then create a number statement using those numbers.

Four thousand ninety
9 tens + 3 thousands + 10 hundreds

4.NBT.2

5. If Cyrus started at 0 and used the rule "add 3" and Caroline started at 9 and used the rule "add 2", who would reach 21 first? Show your work.

4.OA.5

1. Draw a model that is equivalent to $\frac{1}{2}$ but has more than 2 parts.

4.NF.1

2. Write the equation that is modeled below.

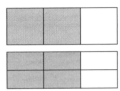

4.NF.1

3. What fraction is modeled below?

4.NF.1

4. Draw a model that is equivalent to $\frac{3}{4}$ but has more than 4 parts.

4.NF.1

5. On Monday Sol earned $112 mowing lawns but spent $13 for gas. On Friday he earned $204 and spent $22 on gas.

   A. How much money did Sol earn on those 2 days?
   B. What were his expenses?
   C. If he didn't earn or spend anything else that week, how much money did Sol get to keep?

4.OA.3

1. Draw a model that is equivalent to $\frac{2}{3}$ but has more than 3 parts.

4.NF.1

2. Write the equation that is modeled below.

4.NF.1

3. Draw a model that is equivalent to $\frac{4}{16}$ but has less than 16 parts.

4.NF.1

4. Write 2 fractions that are equivalent to $\frac{4}{12}$.

4.NF.1

5. Using the digits 4, 5, 1, and 5 exactly once, write a 4-digit number that has one 5 that is 10 times the value of the other 5.

4.NBT.1

1. Write the equation of the model shown below.

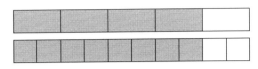

4.NF.1

2. Give 2 other fractions that are equivalent to the model below.

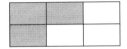

4.NF.1

3. A pattern starts with the number 51 and uses the rule "subtract 4". What are the first 4 numbers after 51?

4.OA.5

4. What "rule" is being used in the set of numbers 13, 17, 21, 25, 29?

4.OA.5

5. If Kris started at 100 and used the rule "subtract 4" and Boris started at 90 and used the rule "subtract 3", who would reach 72 first? Show your work.

4.OA.5

 # DAY 6
CHALLENGE
QUESTION

Kammi started at 9 and used the rule +5. Jackson started at 2(and used the rule +1. Vera started at 12 and used the rule +3. Wh would reach 24 first? Show your work.

4.OA.5

Comparisons are some of what you'll practice in Week 7. You'll have a chance to use the comparison symbols (<, >, =) to make true number sentences that involve fractions and compare them to benchmark fractions like $\frac{1}{4}$, $\frac{1}{2}$ and $\frac{3}{4}$.

You can find detailed video explanations to each problem in the book by visiting:
ArgoPrep.com

---

1. Use the fractions $\frac{1}{2}$ and $\frac{5}{8}$ to write a number sentence using a comparison symbol.

4.NF.2

---

2. The weight of 3 newborn puppies is shown below.

    A. Which puppy weighed the most?
    B. Which puppy weighed the least?

Astro	$\frac{3}{4}$ pound
Dino	$\frac{7}{8}$ pound
Rex	$\frac{3}{5}$ pound

4.NF.2

---

3. Make a drawing that shows $\frac{5}{8} < \frac{4}{6}$.

4.NF.2

---

4. Make a model of 27 divided by 8.

4.NBT.6

---

5. The students had 6 minutes to run as far as they could. The results are shown below.

    A. Who ran the farthest distance?
    B. Who ran the shortest distance?

Austin	$\frac{1}{3}$ mile
Brody	$\frac{5}{8}$ mile
Amber	$\frac{1}{2}$ mile

4.NF.2

1. Make a drawing that shows $\frac{1}{3} > \frac{1}{4}$.

4.NF.2

2. Compare $\frac{2}{5}$ and $\frac{1}{3}$.

    A. What is the Least Common Denominator (LCD) for these 2 fractions?
    B. What are the equivalent fractions using the LCD?
    C. What is the number sentence that compares $\frac{2}{5}$ and $\frac{1}{3}$?

4.NF.2

3. Use the model below to write 2 true number sentences.

4.NF.2

4. Write 2 true number sentences using the fractions $\frac{5}{6}$ and $\frac{3}{4}$.

4.NF.2

5. Joshua drove 5 times as far as Hannah. If Joshua drove 50 miles, how far did Hannah drive?

4.OA.2

1. Use the model below to write 2 true number sentences.

4.NF.2

2. Draw a model to show $\frac{2}{3} > \frac{2}{5}$.

4.NF.2

3. The weight of 3 potatoes is shown below.

A	$\frac{4}{5}$ pound
B	$\frac{5}{8}$ pound
C	$\frac{3}{4}$ pound

A. Which potato weighed the most?
B. Which potato weighed the least?

4.NF.2

4. Compare $\frac{7}{12}$ and $\frac{3}{4}$.

A. What is the Least Common Denominator (LCD) for these 2 fractions?
B. What are the equivalent fractions using the LCD?
C. What is a number sentence that compares $\frac{7}{12}$ and $\frac{3}{4}$?

4.NF.2

5. Erin mowed 4 times as much lawn as Bethany. If Bethany mowed B amount of lawn, what is an equation that can be used to find E, the amount of lawn mowed by Erin?

4.OA.2

WEEK 7 · DAY 4

1. Use the fractions $\frac{2}{3}$ and $\frac{3}{4}$ to write a 2 true number sentences.

4.NF.2

---

2. Compare $\frac{1}{2}$ and $\frac{5}{11}$.

    A. What is the Least Common Denominator (LCD) for these 2 fractions?
    B. What are the equivalent fractions using the LCD?
    C. What is the number sentence that compares $\frac{1}{2}$ and $\frac{5}{11}$?

4.NF.2

---

3. The amount of juice some students drank is shown below.

Michelle	$\frac{1}{4}$ cup
Brock	$\frac{1}{5}$ cup
Amanda	$\frac{1}{8}$ cup

    A. Who drank the most?
    B. Who drank the least?

4.NF.2

---

4. Larry sold 412 golf balls for $2 each and 309 basketballs for $7 each. How much money did he receive for selling the golf and basketballs?

4.OA.3

---

5. Compare $\frac{3}{8}$ and $\frac{5}{12}$.

    A. What is the Least Common Denominator (LCD) for these 2 fractions?
    B. What are the equivalent fractions using the LCD?
    C. What is the number sentence that compares $\frac{3}{8}$ and $\frac{5}{12}$?

4.NF.2

1. What 2 number sentences are modeled below?

4.NF.2

2. Use the fractions $\frac{4}{5}$ and $\frac{5}{6}$ to write a 2 true number sentences.

4.NF.2

3. Draw a model to show $\frac{3}{4} < \frac{7}{8}$.

4.NF.2

4. What factors do 12 and 18 **both** have?

4.OA.4

5. Compare $\frac{5}{6}$ and $\frac{8}{9}$.

    A. What is the Least Common Denominator (LCD) for these 2 fractions?
    B. What are the equivalent fractions using the LCD?
    C. What is the number sentence that compares $\frac{5}{6}$ and $\frac{8}{9}$?

4.NF.2

DAY 6
CHALLENGE
QUESTION

Draw models that show $\frac{2}{5}$, $\frac{1}{3}$ and $\frac{7}{15}$ 4.NF.2

Put the fractions in order from smallest to largest.

48

Week 8 allows you to work with the addition and subtraction of like fractions, fractions that have the same denominator. It will build on what you practiced last week by offering chances to work with equivalent fractions and mixed numbers.

You can find detailed video explanations to each problem in the book by visiting: ArgoPrep.com

WEEK 8 · DAY I

ARGOPREP.COM

1. Noel needs $\frac{1}{3}$ cup of butter for one loaf. She will make 8 loaves.

   A. How many cups of butter will she need?

   B. If she started with $\frac{12}{3}$ cups of butter, how many cups will remain?

   4.NF.3

2. Noel's recipe made 5 $\frac{1}{8}$ pounds of brownies. If her sister ate 1 $\frac{3}{8}$ pounds, how many pounds of brownies were left?

   4.NF.3

3. Lincoln worked on his car for 3 $\frac{3}{4}$ hours on Friday and 5 hours on Saturday. How much time did he work on his car?

   4.NF.3

4. There are 44 students in band. Each van can hold 9 students to take to the competition.

   A. How many vans will be needed?
   B. How many students will be in the last van?

   4.NBT.6

5. If Tammy walks $\frac{4}{5}$ of a mile each day, how many miles will she walk in 1 week?

   4.NF.3

6. Make an addition problem that has $\frac{4}{7}$ as a sum and uses only $\frac{1}{7}$ as addends.

   4.NF.3

1. The beverages are shown below.

Coffee	$8 \frac{2}{9}$ gallons
Tea	14 gallons
Lemonade	$11 \frac{7}{9}$ gallons

    A. How much more tea is there than coffee?
    B. How many gallons of drink are there altogether?
    C. How much more lemonade is there than coffee?

4.NF.3

2. Addison ran $8 \frac{1}{3}$ miles. Rose ran $1 \frac{1}{3}$ miles farther. How far did Rose run?

4.NF.3

3. A pattern starts with the number 87 and uses the rule "subtract 4". What are the first 4 numbers after 83?

4.OA.5

4. Write an addition number sentence for the drawing below.

4.NF.3

5. The board was $4 \frac{3}{8}$ feet long. Bruce needed a $5 \frac{1}{8}$ foot board. How much longer does the board need to be?

4.NF.3

1. Allie's pumpkin weighed 12 $\frac{3}{4}$ pounds. Annie's pumpkin weighed 15 pounds.

   A. How many more pounds did Annie's pumpkin weigh?
   B. How many pounds did the pumpkins weigh altogether?

   4.NF.3

2. Caroline and 4 of her friends each ate $\frac{2}{4}$ cup of yogurt.

   A. How much did they eat altogether?
   B. If there was $\frac{17}{4}$ cups of yogurt to start, how much was left?

   4.NF.3

3. Each car requires $\frac{4}{5}$ gallons of gas to start. How much gas must be available if Stan wants to start 20 cars?

   4.NF.3

4. Write an addition sentence for the drawing below.

   4.NF.3

5. Gloria inherited $14,965. Round this number to the thousands and the tens places.

   4.NBT.3

ARGOPREP.COM

1. It took Devin $4\frac{3}{8}$ hours to drive to college and then another $1\frac{5}{8}$ hours to drive to a friend's house. How many hours was Devin driving?

4.NF.3

2. Draw a model that shows $\frac{1}{10} + \frac{1}{10} + \frac{1}{10} + \frac{1}{10} = \frac{4}{10}$

4.NF.3

3. Write an addition sentence for the model below.

4.NF.3

4. Write 2 fractions that are equivalent to $\frac{4}{12}$.

4.NF.1

5. The jumbo jet had 351 passengers. At the first airport, 198 passengers disembarked and 75 new passengers got on. Now how many people are on the plane? Show your work.

4.NBT.4

1. Dale bought $\frac{4}{5}$ pounds of peanuts each week. How many pounds of peanuts did he have after 6 weeks?

4.NF.3

2. Draw a model that shows $\frac{7}{8} + \frac{7}{8} + \frac{7}{8} = \frac{21}{8}$.

4.NF.3

3. Each week Brutus ate $15\frac{3}{4}$ cups of dog food and Zeb ate $21\frac{2}{4}$ cups.

   A. How much food did the dogs eat each week?
   B. How much more food did Zeb eat than Brutus each week?

4.NF.3

4. Kaley had 80 dollars and Edward had 8 dollars. How many times more money did Kaley have?

4.NBT.1

5. Write an addition sentence for the drawing below.

4.NF.3

DAY 6
CHALLENGE
QUESTION

Darby weighed $10\frac{3}{5}$ pounds less than Clarise. If Darby weighed $56\frac{1}{5}$ pounds, how much did Clarise weigh?

4.NF.3

54

Fractions this week are being multiplied by whole numbers. You will begin to see how fractions are used in the real world and how they apply to word problems.

You can find detailed video explanations to each problem in the book by visiting:
ArgoPrep.com

1. If each bee can make $\frac{1}{4}$ quart of honey, how many quarts do 9 bees make?

4.NF.4

2. Each of the 7 ball players drank $\frac{5}{6}$ gallon of water. How much water did the players drink altogether?

4.NF.4

3. Write a multiplication number sentence for the model below.

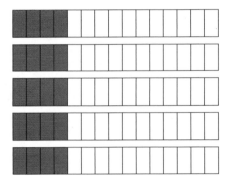

4.NF.4

4. Write an addition sentence for the model above.

4.NF.3

5. Every day last week it rained $\frac{2}{3}$ inches of rain. How much rain was there last week?

4.NF.4

1. Each street sign requires $\frac{2}{3}$ yard of sidewalk. If there are 8 signs, how much sidewalk must there be?

4.NF.4

2. If there are 3 children and each child picks $\frac{3}{4}$ bucket of blueberries, how many buckets of blueberries will be picked?

4.NF.4

3. Write a multiplication sentence for the model below.

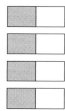

4.NF.4

4. There were $2\frac{4}{5}$ granola bars until Harold ate $1\frac{3}{5}$ of them. Now how many granola bars are there?

4.NF.3

5. The tractor could mow $\frac{4}{7}$ of an acre in 1 hour. How many acres could the tractor mow in 8 hours?

4.NF.4

ARGOPREP.COM

---

1. Write a multiplication sentence for the model below.

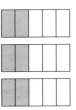

4.NF.4

---

2. Each book weighs $\frac{7}{8}$ of a kilogram. How much do 9 books weigh?

4.NF.4

---

3. If each apple weighed $\frac{1}{2}$ of a pound, how much would 7 apples weigh?

4.NF.4

---

4. The race was $\frac{4}{5}$ kilometer long. How far would a racer go in 8 races?

4.NF.4

---

5. Bella drank 12 glasses of water during the day. Bella drank 3 times as many glasses as Rose. How many glasses of water did Rose drink?

4.OA.2

1. Jasmine exercises for $\frac{3}{4}$ of an hour each day. How much time does she spend exercising in 5 days?

4.NF.4

2. Dara can swim a lap in $\frac{9}{10}$ of a minute. How long would 5 laps take?

4.NF.4

3. Colby drank $\frac{3}{8}$ cup of juice per hour for 3 hours. How much juice did Colby drink?

4.NF.4

4. Write a number sentence for the model below.

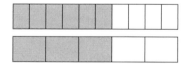

4.NF.1

5. Chester could eat $\frac{1}{3}$ of a can of tuna in a minute. How much tuna could he eat in 5 minutes?

4.NF.4

1. Becky talked on the phone for $\frac{3}{5}$ of an hour one day. If she did the same for a total of 6 days, how much time would she have spent on the phone?

    4.NF.4

2. Each slice of cake gets $\frac{1}{2}$ cup of ice cream. How much ice cream would 15 slices get?

    4.NF.4

3. Dominic practiced for $\frac{1}{4}$ hour each evening. How much time would he practice over 5 evenings?

    4.NF.4

4. What 2 number sentences are modeled below?

    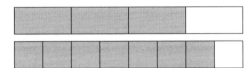

    4.NF.2

5. Write a multiplication number sentence for the model below.

    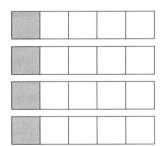

    4.NF.4

DAY 6
CHALLENGE QUESTION

Janie ran $\frac{6}{5}$ of a mile for 4 days. Robert ran $\frac{4}{5}$ of a mile for 7 days. Who ran the furthest distance and by how much?

4.NF.4

The fractions in Week 10 focus on those fractions that have 10 or 100 in the denominator. These fractions can be added together and you'll also have a chance to rewrite these fractions as a decimal number.

You can find detailed video explanations to each problem in the book by visiting: ArgoPrep.com

1. Omar is adding up $\frac{4}{10}$ and $\frac{7}{100}$ of a dollar. How much money is that? Express your answer as a fraction.

4.NF.5

For questions 2–3, use $\frac{5}{10}$ and $\frac{10}{100}$.

2. Rewrite these two fractions so that

   A. they both are fractions with 10 in the denominator and
   B. they both are fractions with a denominator of 100.

4.NF.5

3. If the 2 fractions above were added, what would be the sum?

4.NF.5

4. Erica read $\frac{3}{100}$ of her book on one day and $\frac{7}{10}$ on another day. How much of her book did she read on those 2 days? Express as a fraction.

4.NF.5

5. The chart below shows the number of chairs in 3 sections of an auditorium.

Section A	4,908
Section B	1,744
Section C	2,356

   A. How many seats are there in Sections A, B and C?
   B. How many more seats are there in Section A than in Section C?

4.NBT.4

1. Cale had 2 strings that were $\frac{3}{10}$ and $\frac{14}{100}$ of an inch long. How long were the pieces if put together?

4.NF.5

2. Shelly spent $\frac{2}{100}$ and $\frac{5}{10}$ of an hour knitting. How much time did Shelly spend knitting?

4.NF.5

3. Joanne ordered $\frac{9}{100}$ of a yard of calico and $\frac{3}{10}$ of a yard of paisley. How much material did Joanne order?

4.NF.5

4. Look at the drawing below.

A. What is an addition sentence that is being modeled?
B. What is a multiplication sentence that is being modeled?

4.NF.3
4.NF.4

5. The amount of snow that Ketchikan, Alaska received last week was $\frac{8}{10}$ of a foot. If there was $\frac{3}{100}$ of a foot today, what would the total snowfall be?

4.NF.5

1. Hunter had $\frac{19}{100}$ of an inch cut from her hair in May, then another 2/10 of an inch in June. How much hair did she have cut in May and June?

4.NF.5

2. Lynnette colors $\frac{57}{100}$ of the page and Harper colors $\frac{4}{10}$ of the page. Rewrite the fractions as decimals.

4.NF.6

3. Write a number sentence that compares the 2 models below.

4.NF.1

4. The tree grew 6/10 of an inch. Write 6/10 as a decimal.

4.NF.6

5. The ant carried $\frac{13}{100}$ of an ounce. Write $\frac{13}{100}$ as a decimal.

4.NF.6

1. The roller coaster took $\frac{8}{10}$ of a minute to go up the hill. Write $\frac{8}{10}$ as a decimal.

4.NF.6

2. The grass grew $\frac{46}{100}$ of an inch. Write $\frac{46}{100}$ as a decimal.

4.NF.6

3. Write a multiplication number sentence for the model below.

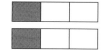

4.NF.4

4. The board was $\frac{89}{100}$ of a yard. Write $\frac{89}{100}$ as a decimal.

4.NF.6

5. There was $\frac{33}{100}$ of a minute difference between first and second place in the race. Write $\frac{33}{100}$ as a decimal.

4.NF.6

1. He read 6/100 of the newspaper. Write 6/100 as a decimal.

4.NF.6

2. Megan biked $\frac{2}{10}$ of a mile and swam $\frac{21}{100}$ of a mile. How far did she travel?

4.NF.5

3. Zoe jumped 70/100 of a yard and then she jumped another 2/10 of a yard. How many yards did Zoe jump altogether?

4.NF.5

4. Charles wrote $\frac{51}{100}$ of his paper. Write $\frac{51}{100}$ as a decimal.

4.NF.6

Use the drawing below to answer questions 5–6.

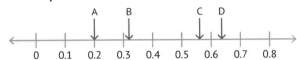

5. Which point most likely is located at $\frac{63}{100}$?

4.NF.6

6. Which point most likely is located at $\frac{20}{100}$?

4.NF.6

DAY 6
CHALLENGE QUESTION

Joel grew $\frac{2}{10}$ of an inch in June, $\frac{17}{100}$ of an inch in July and $\frac{1}{10}$ of an inch in August. How much did Joel grow over the summer? Write your answer as a decimal.

4.NF.5

Last week you learned about writing decimal numbers. This week you will have an opportunity to compare these numbers using the comparison symbols <, >, and =.

You can find detailed video explanations to each problem in the book by visiting:
ArgoPrep.com

1. The oak tree grew 0.3 inches. The pine tree grew 0.27 inches. Use the 2 decimal numbers to create a number sentence using a comparison symbol.

4.NF.7

2. Use the model below to write a number sentence using decimals.

4.NF.7

3. The ant was 0.09 inches and the worm was 0.9 inches. Use the 2 decimal numbers to create a number sentence using a comparison symbol.

4.NF.7

4. Round 117,542 to the nearest hundred and hundred thousand.

4.NBT.3

5. The amount of rainfall in inches is shown below.

Day 1	0.4
Day 2	0.16
Day 3	0.61

Place the days in order based upon their amount of rainfall. The least amount of rain should be first.

4.NF.7

1. Todd rode 0.94 of a mile and then 0.98 of a mile. Use the 2 decimal numbers to create a number sentence using a comparison symbol.

4.NF.7

2. The thickness of 3 coins is shown below in centimeters.

Coin A	0.7
Coin B	0.17
Coin C	0.07

Place the coins in order based upon their thickness. The thinnest should be listed first.

4.NF.7

3. Which number has more factors 15 or 25? Show your work.

4.OA.4

4. Use the model below to write a number sentence using decimals.

4.NF.7

5. Change $\frac{8}{10}$ and $\frac{74}{100}$ to decimals and use them to write a true number sentence.

4.NF.7

---

1. Ted measured out 0.1 teaspoon of sugar and then 0.01 teaspoon of salt. Use the 2 decimal numbers to create a number sentence comparing the numbers.

4.NF.7

---

2. Change $\frac{42}{100}$ and $\frac{5}{10}$ to decimals and use them to write a number sentence.

4.NF.7

---

3. The chart below shows the length of 3 trails in kilometers.

Overland	0.15
Dutch Pass	0.51
Lookout	0.05

Place the trails in order from shortest to longest.

4.NF.7

---

4. The church bought 25 sets of candles. Each set costs $49. How much did all of the candles cost?

4.NBT.5

---

5. Use the model below to write a number sentence using decimals.

4.NF.7

1. Lorelei measured 2 toothpicks. One was 0.39 cm and one was 0.7 cm. Use the 2 numbers to create a number sentence comparing them.

4.NF.7

2. Change $\frac{2}{10}$ and $\frac{58}{100}$ to decimals and use them to write a number sentence.

4.NF.7

3. Use the model below to write a number sentence using decimals.

4.NF.7

4. Using only 9 and 3 as factors, what are the first 4 multiples of these factors?

4.OA.4

5. Susan walked 0.6 km and then walked 0.49 km. Use the 2 decimal numbers to create a number sentence comparing the numbers.

4.NF.7

1. Change $\frac{32}{100}$ and $\frac{3}{10}$ to decimals and use them to write a number sentence using a comparison symbol.

   4.NF.7

2. The material needed for some clothing is shown below in yards.

socks	0.8
belt	0.3
hat	0.65

   Put the clothing in order from the least amount of material needed to the most.

   4.NF.7

3. Use the model below to write a number sentence using decimals.

   4.NF.7

4. One recipe called for 0.71 cup of flour and 0.07 cup of baking soda. Use the 2 decimal numbers to create a number sentence using a comparison symbol.

   4.NF.7

5. Dwight lost $\frac{7}{8}$ of a pound then gained $\frac{4}{8}$ of a pound and lost another $\frac{3}{8}$ of a pound. How much weight did he lose overall?

   4.NF.3

DAY 6
CHALLENGE QUESTION

Mrs. Grande measured the thickness of her yarns. They were $\frac{44}{100}$ mm, $\frac{3}{10}$ mm, and $\frac{7}{100}$ mm thick. Change these measurements to decimal numbers and then list them from the thinnest to the thickest.

4.NF.7

Inches, feet, yards and miles — all of these measurement units and many others will be used in Week 12 exercises. This week you'll work on changing from one unit of measure to another. But be careful — make sure you know whether you are using metric units or other units!

You can find detailed video explanations to each problem in the book by visiting:
ArgoPrep.com

1. The distance to school is 3 miles.

    A. How many yards to school?
    B. How many feet to school?

4.MD.1

2. Look at the chart below. What numbers are missing?

Meters	Centimeters
1	100
3	300

Write an ordered pair that would complete the chart above.

4.MD.1

3. The race was a 5K, also known as 5 kilometers.

    A. How many meters long is the race?
    B. How many times longer is the race than 1000 meters?

4.MD.1

4. A football field is 100 yards long.

    A. Write an equation to find F, the number of feet in the length of a football field.
    B. How many feet is the length of a football field?

4.MD.1

5. Draw a shape pattern that shows the rule "subtract 3".

4.OA.5

1. How many times longer is 1 foot than 1 inch? Explain your answer.

4.MD.1

2. The office building was 45 meters tall. How many centimeters tall was the building?

4.MD.1

3. Find an ordered pair that completes the table below.

Centimeters	Millimeters
10	100
30	300

4.MD.1

4. Mrs. Boyd bought 4 pounds of grapes.

    A. Write an equation to find W, the weight of the grapes in ounces.
    B. How many ounces are in 4 pounds of grapes?

4.MD.1

5. Which product is larger (2,091 × 3) or (75 × 84)? Show your work.

4.NBT.5

ARGOPREP.COM

---

1. Find an ordered pair that completes the table below.

Hours	Minutes
1	60
3	180

4.MD.1

---

2. Grandma's house is 97 kilometers from us. How many meters away is Grandma's house?

4.MD.1

---

3. The mass of the fire extinguisher was 9 kilograms. What is the mass of the extinguisher in grams?

4.MD.1

---

4. The contestant had 4 minutes to answer all the questions. How many seconds did the contestant have?

4.MD.1

---

5. What number is missing in the table below?

Feet	Inches
1	12
3	
5	60

4.MD.1

1. The top of the roof was 16 yards.

   A. Write an equation that shows R, the height of the roof in feet.
   B. How many feet tall was the top of the roof?

4.MD.1

2. Darlene had 4 days to find a dress. How many hours did she have?

4.MD.1

3. Luke jumped 7 meters and Leila jumped 698 centimeters. Who jumped farther? Show your work.

4.MD.1

4. Melanie brought three 2-liter bottles of soda to the party. How many milliliters of soda did Melanie bring?

4.MD.1

5. For the race, each runner had to run $\frac{2}{3}$ of a mile. If there were 8 runners on a team, how long was the race?

4.NF.4

6. Rachael is 6 feet tall. How many inches tall is Rachael?

4.MD.1

1. Find an ordered pair that completes the table below.

Yards	Feet
1	3
3	9

4.MD.

2. The candle was 2 kilograms.

   A. Write an equation to find C, the number of grams of the candle.
   B. How many grams was the candle?

4.MD.

3. Ainsley bought 5 pounds of fudge. How many ounces of fudge did she have?

4.MD.1

4. The distance to the neighbor's house is 2 meters. The distance to the mall is 2 kilometers. How many times farther is it to the mall than to the neighbor's house?

4.MD.1

5. The soccer game lasted 2 hours. How many minutes was the soccer game?

4.MD.1

DAY 6
CHALLENGE
QUESTION

The bike trail was 8 kilometers. How many centimeters was the trail? Show your work.

4.MD.1

78

WEEK 13

It gets real in Week 13. You will use all kinds of operations (adding, subtracting, multiplying and/or dividing) to solve word problems that use measurements such as units for time, money, length, area, and perimeter in the real world.

You can find detailed video explanations to each problem in the book by visiting:
ArgoPrep.com

1. The garage door was 8 feet. The house door was 96 inches. Which door was taller? Show your work.

   4.MD.2

2. The road trip was supposed to take 16 hours. They have already driven 375 minutes. How much further do they have to go?

   4.MD.2

3. In the 5-kilometer race, Brandi had already run 2 kilometers. How many meters did she have yet to run?

   4.MD.2

4. Nathan is 3 feet tall. His brother is 33 inches tall. Who was taller? Show your work.

   4.MD.2

5. Mr. Evans cooked his turkey for 5 hours and Mrs. Tryon cooked hers for 270 minutes. Who cooked the turkey longer? Show your work.

   4.MD.2

6. The truck put down rock on 3 kilometers of the road. Wyatt put down rock on 1,106 meters of the road. How much rock did the truck and Wyatt put down in meters? Show your work.

   4.MD.2

WEEK 13 · DAY 2

ARGOPREP.COM

1. Max spent 3 hours on his project and Jackson spent 200 minutes on his project.

   A. How many minutes did they spend altogether on the project?
   B. How many more minutes did Jackson spend than Max?

   4.MD.2

2. The red marker was 25 centimeters long and the blue marker was 260 millimeters long. Which marker was longer? Show your work.

   4.MD.2

3. There was about 4 days worth of work for the team to do. If they split up the time among 8 workers, how many hours would each worker need to work?

   4.MD.2

4. Mrs. Varga bought 56 ounces of ham and 4 pounds of beef.

   A. Which meat did Mrs. Varga buy more of?
   B. What is the difference in the amounts of meat?

   4.MD.2

5. Joy talked on the phone for 175 minutes and Caleb talked on his phone for 3 hours. Who talked longer? Show your work.

   4.MD.2

6. What is the smallest 4-digit number that could round to 7,500 if we round to the nearest hundred?

   4.NBT.3

1. The rectangle below has an area of 48 square meters. What is its perimeter?

12 meters

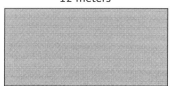

4.MD.3

2. There is a garden that is 8 yards wide and has an area of 104 yards^2.

A. What is the length?
B. What is the perimeter?

4.MD.3

3. A sidewalk was being poured. It had an area of 120 square feet and a width of 5 feet. What was its perimeter?

4.MD.3

4. A deck is shown below. The perimeter is 68 feet. What is the area?

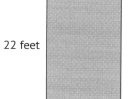

22 feet

4.MD.3

5. Each chicken was fed $\frac{1}{8}$ cup of food. There are 13 chickens.

A. Write an equation to show how to find the amount of food, F.
B. How much food was needed?

4.NF.4

6. There was a trampoline that had a perimeter of 60 feet with a width of 15 feet.

A. What was the length of the trampoline?
B. What was the trampoline's area?

4.MD.3

1. A stage is shown below. It has a perimeter of 62 feet.

14 feet

A. What is the length?
B. What is its area?

4.MD.3

2. Beatrice wants to enclose a run for her dog. The area she wants to enclose is 144 meters² and has a width of 9 meters.

A. How long is the length of the area?
B. How much fencing will she need?

4.MD.3

3. Below is a game board. It has a perimeter of 62 inches.

What is the area of the game board?

18 in

4.MD.3

4. The Wilsons have a pool that is 10 feet wide and the border around the pool is 44 feet.

A. What is the length of the pool?
B. What is the area of the pool?

4.MD.3

5. The rectangle below has a width of 7 cm and an area of 105 cm².

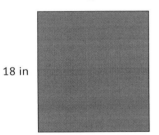

7 cm

A. What is the length?
B. What is the perimeter of the rectangle?

4.MD.3

6. Which has more factor pairs 56 or 99? Show your work.

4.OA.4

1. Ruth drank 810 mL of water in the morning and 1300 mL of water in the afternoon. Tin drank 2L of water. Who drank more water? Show your work.

4.MD.2

2. Tinley took measurements of her driveway but then lost some of the numbers. Wha numbers would complete the chart below?

Length	Width	Perimeter	Area
	10 feet	68 feet	

4.MD.3

3. Tony had a rug that needed a new border. The rug had an area of 80 ft² and a width of 8 feet. How much border would he need?

4.MD.3

Below is a chart that shows how long some students studied. Use the information to answer question 4–5.

Aaron	200 minutes
Tori	2.5 hours
Alyssa	4 hours, 10 minutes

4. How much time did the students study altogether?

4.MD.2

5. What fraction of the day is that amount of time?

4.MD.3

DAY 6
CHALLENGE QUESTION

Below is a drawing of a pool and its deck. The deck has an area of 45 square meters.

A. What is the area of the pool?

B. What is the perimeter of the pool?

5 m

17 m

4.MD.3

WEEK 14

ARGOPREP.COM

VIDEO EXPLANATIONS

Like to draw or look at pictures? If so, you'll love Week 14! Here you will see and use information that is given in tables or shown on charts. Be sure to read all of the titles and information given to help you understand what the numbers mean.

You can find detailed video explanations to each problem in the book by visiting:
ArgoPrep.com

1. Take the data below and create a dot plot.

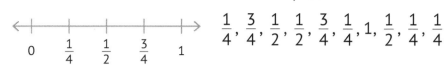

$$\frac{1}{4}, \frac{3}{4}, \frac{1}{2}, \frac{1}{2}, \frac{3}{4}, \frac{1}{4}, 1, \frac{1}{2}, \frac{1}{4}, \frac{1}{4}$$

4.MD.4

Jerica measured the daily amounts of rainfall and her results are shown below. Use her results to answer questions 2-4.

Rainfall (inches)

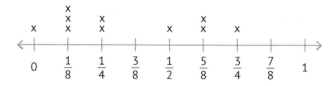

2. How many days did Jerica measure the rainfall?

4.MD.4

3. **A.** What was the largest amount received on any one day?
   B. What was the smallest amount received on any one day?

4.MD.4

4. How many more days had $\frac{1}{8}$ of an inch than had $\frac{5}{8}$ of an inch?

4.MD.4

5. Use the number line below.

   A. What are the 2 numbers as fractions shown on the number line?
   B. What are the 2 numbers as decimals shown on the number line?

4.NF.6

6. There was a square that had an area of 64 square centimeters. What was the perimeter of that square?

4.MD.4

he amount of water each tennis player drank is shown below. Use the information to answer
uestions 1–3.

Water (gallons)

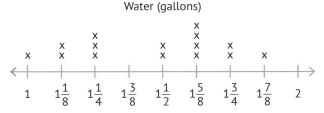

1. How many players were on the team?

4.MD.4

2. What is the difference between the largest and the smallest amounts of water the players
drank?

4.MD.4

3. How much water did the team drink?

4.MD.4

s. Jamora's class collected food for the food bank. The amount each student collected is shown
elow. Use the information to answer questions 4–6.

Food Donated (pounds)

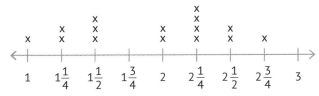

4. What was the largest amount of food any one student donated?

4.MD.4

5. How many more students donated $2\frac{1}{4}$ pounds than donated 1 pound?

4.MD.4

6. How many students donated MORE than 2 pounds?

4.MD.4

1. Write an equation that shows what 6 times greater than 12 is.

4.OA.

The amount of time per week that some students spent using a phone is shown below. Use the information to answer questions 2–5.

Time Spent on Phone (hours)

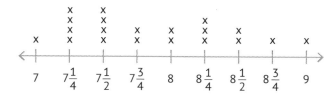

2. **A.** What unit is being used to measure the time?
   B. How many students' phone time was measured?

4.MD.4

3. What is the largest amount of time shown by this data set?

4.MD.4

4. How many students talked LESS than 8 hours a week?

4.MD.4

5. How many fewer students talk 8 $\frac{3}{4}$ hours than talk 7 $\frac{1}{4}$ hours?

4.MD.4

6. What are all the factor pairs for 45?

4.OA.4

ARGOPREP.COM

The plot below represents the cups of soup that some students had for lunch. Use it to answer questions 1–3.

1. How many cups of soup did the class eat?

4.MD.4

2. How many students ate $\frac{1}{4}$ cup of soup?

4.MD.4

3. Which amount did the most students eat?

4.MD.4

4. Donovan had 10 times as many rubber bands as Liz. If Liz had 4 bands, how many did Donovan have?

4.NBT.1

5. The birth weights of some babies is shown below.

Weight (pounds)	Number of babies
7	5
$7\frac{1}{4}$	3
$7\frac{1}{2}$	2
$7\frac{3}{4}$	5

Create a dot plot to show this information.

4.MD.4

Some students' shoe sizes are shown below. Use the data to answer questions 1–5.

Students' Shoe Sizes

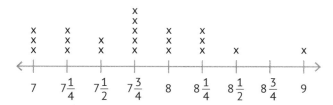

1. How many students had their shoe size recorded?

4.MD.4

2. What size did no student have?

4.MD.4

3. How many LESS students had size 8 $\frac{1}{2}$ than had size 7 $\frac{1}{4}$?

4.MD.4

4. Which size did more students have than any other size?

4.MD.4

5. How many MORE students had size 7 $\frac{3}{4}$ than had size 9?

4.MD.4

DAY 6
CHALLENGE
QUESTION

Use the set of numbers 99, 88, 77... to answer the questions below.

A. What "rule" is being used?

B. What would be the next number in the set?

4.OA.5

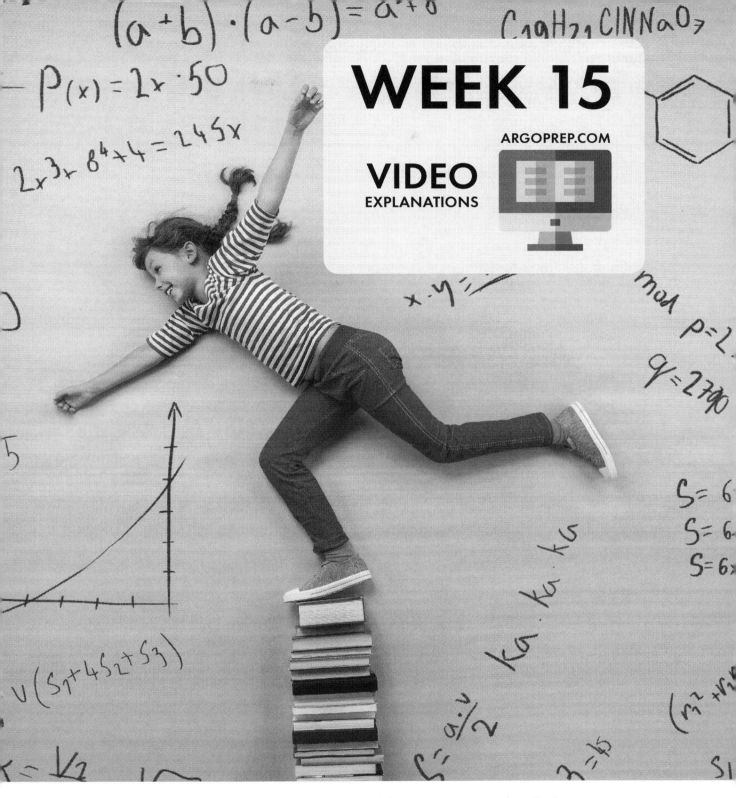

WEEK 15

ARGOPREP.COM

VIDEO EXPLANATIONS

Angles, angles and more angles for Week 15! You'll be able to measure angles, find missing measures, and use circles to understand what "piece" of a circle a certain angle is.

You can find detailed video explanations to each problem in the book by visiting:
ArgoPrep.com

1. Angle T turns through 77 one-degree angles. What is the measure of Angle T?

4.MD.5

2. The degrees of certain angles are shown below.

Degrees	Angle
360	Whole circle
	$\frac{1}{4}$ of a circle
	$\frac{1}{2}$ of a circle
	$\frac{1}{10}$ of a circle

Fill in the correct degrees to complete the chart.

4.MD.5

3. Each angle in this hexagon is 1/6 of a circle. What is the measure of one angle?

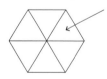

4.MD.5

4. Make a model of 56 divided by 5.

4.NBT.6

5. Angle U turns through 321 one-degree angles. What is the measure of Angle U?

4.MD.5

1. Angle M turns through 275 one-degree angles. What is the measure of Angle M?

4.MD.5

2. Colleen biked 7 times as far as Anthony. If Anthony biked 14 miles, how many miles did Colleen bike?

4.OA.2

3. How many degrees are in an angle that is 1/12 of a circle?

4.MD.5

4. Each angle in this octagon is $\frac{1}{8}$ of a circle. What is the measure of one angle?

4.MD.5

5. Angle G turns through 103 one-degree angles. What is the measure of Angle G?

4.MD.5

6. What is the measure of the angle formed by the 2 books below?

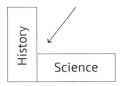

4.MD.5

1. What is the measure of an angle created by $\frac{1}{2}$ of a circle as shown below?

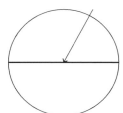

4.MD.5

2. The degrees of certain angles are shown below.

Fill in the correct degrees to complete the chart.

Degrees	Angle
360	Whole circle
	$\frac{1}{3}$ of a circle
	$\frac{1}{6}$ of a circle
	$\frac{1}{12}$ of a circle

4.MD.5

3. Toddler Kayla is 0.86 meters tall. Write 0.86 as a fraction.

4.NF.6

4. Each angle in this square is $\frac{1}{4}$ of a circle. What is the measure of one angle?

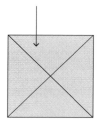

4.MD.5

5. Angle Q turns through 117 one-degree angles. What is the measure of Angle Q?

4.MD.5

1. Angle L is $\frac{1}{5}$ of a circle. How many degrees is Angle L?

4.MD.5

2. Find the measure of the angle indicated below.

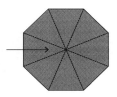

4.MD.5

3. Angle K turns through 135 one-degree angles. What is the measure of Angle K?

4.MD.5

4. Mallory was 5 feet 4 inches tall. How many inches tall was she?

4.MD.1

5. Find the measure of Angle B below.

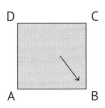

4.MD.5

6. Each bag contains $\frac{3}{5}$ pound of onions. There are 11 bags.

    A. Write a multiplication equation to find the total number of pounds of onions, *P*.
    B. How many pounds of onions are in the bags?

4.NF.4

1. The angle formed by a wall of the house and the ground is shown below. What is the measure of the angle formed by the wall and ground?

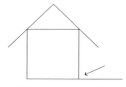

4.MD.

2. Angle S turns through 259 one-degree angles. How many degrees is Angle S?

4.MD.

3. Angle H is formed by $\frac{1}{10}$ of a circle. What is the measurement of Angle H?

4.MD.

4. What factors do 18 and 21 **both** have?

4.OA.4

5. Below is a pentagon that has equal angles. What is the measure of one angle formed by the pentagon?

4.MD.5

6. What is the measure of the angle formed by a pole and a street sign?

4.MD.5

 # DAY 6
CHALLENGE
QUESTION

Place the following angles in order from smallest to largest. Show your reasoning.

Angle A is formed by $\frac{1}{3}$ of a circle.

Angle B turns through 186 one-degree angles.

Angle C is the inside corner of a square.

4.MD.5

Week 16 is additional practice with angles. You'll have lots of opportunities to measure angles that are given and also to think about how you would make an angle if you were given its degrees.

You can find detailed video explanations to each problem in the book by visiting:
ArgoPrep.com

WEEK 16 · DAY 1

ARGOPREP.COM

---

1. Using the figure below, measure to find how many degrees Angles J and K are.

4.MD.6

---

2. Using the figure below, how many degrees are Angles A and B?

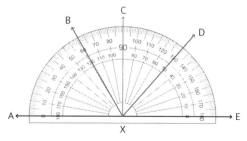

4.MD.6

---

3. Use the protractor below to answer the questions below.

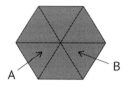

A. How many degrees is Angle AXB?
B. How many degrees is Angle EXD?

4.MD.6

---

4. Use the numbers 871 and 465 to answe the questions below.

A. What is the sum of the 2 numbers?
B. What is the difference of the numbers?

4.NBT.

---

5. What is the measure of the roof angl shown below?

4.MD.6

---

6. Use the number set ... 68, 65, 62, 59 to answer the questions.

A. What is the "rule" for the number set?
B. What number would be next in the set?

4.OA.5

Use the protractor below to answer questions 1 – 2.

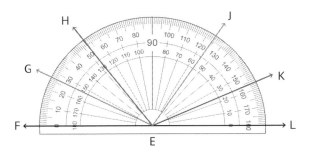

3. How many degrees is the angle indicated below?

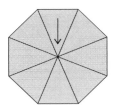

4.MD.6

1. A. What is the measure of Angle FEJ?
B. What is the measure of Angle LEF?

4.MD.6

4. Sketch an angle that is 90° and one that is 45°.

4.MD.6

2. A. How many degrees is Angle HEF?
B. How many degrees is Angle LEK?

4.MD.6

5. Measure the figure below with a protractor. How many degrees are Angles C and D?

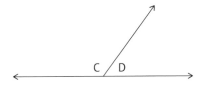

4.MD.6

6. How much larger is the 2 in 2,386 than the 2 in 4,290?

4.NBT.1

Use the protractor below to answer questions 1–2.

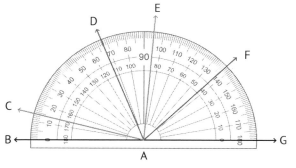

3. Vance spent $18,253 on a car. Round thi number to the ten thousands and th hundreds places.

4.NBT.3

1. A. What is the measure of Angle GAD?
   B. What is the measure of Angle CAB?

4.MD.6

4. Measure the figures below with protractor, how many degrees are Angle G and H?

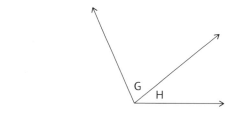

4.MD.6

2. A. How many degrees is Angle DAG?
   B. How many degrees is Angle FAB?

4.MD.6

5. Draw 2 angles. Angle E should measure 170° and Angle F should measure 10°.

4.MD.6

se the drawing below to answer questions
– 3.

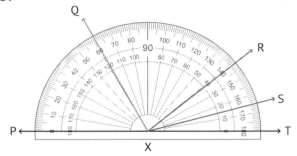

4. What is the measure of the angle indicated below?

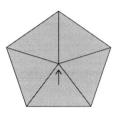

4.MD.6

1. How many degrees is Angle RXT?

4.MD.6

5. Using the figure below, how many degrees are Angles U and V?

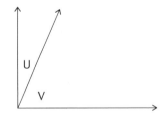

4.MD.6

2. How many degrees is Angle PXQ?

4.MD.6

3. How many degrees is Angle PXT?

4.MD.6

6. What are 2 different equations that can be used to rewrite $\frac{7}{4}$?

4.NF.3
4.NF.4

Use the drawing below to answer questions 1–4.

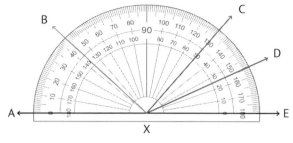

4. How many degrees is Angle AXE?

4.MD.6

1. What does Angle AXB measure?

4.MD.6

5. Write $\frac{7}{10}$ and $\frac{53}{100}$ as decimal numbers. Then use those decimal numbers to write a comparison number sentence.

4.NF.6
4.NF.7

2. What does Angle EXC measure?

4.MD.6

6. Draw Angle H so that it measures 125 degrees.

3. How many degrees is Angle AXC?

4.MD.6

4.MD.6

DAY 6
CHALLENGE QUESTION

Use the protractor below to find 2 angles that equal 90° when added together. Show your work.

4.NF.7

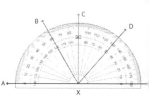

Week 17 works with multiple angles to add them up or separate them. You'll use this information to find missing angle measures.

You can find detailed video explanations to each problem in the book by visiting:
ArgoPrep.com

1. Angle RPQ is 34° and Angle NPQ is 50°. What is the measure of Angle RPN?

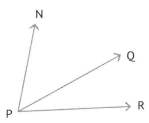

4.MD.7

4. If Angle ACE + Angle ECB = 285° and Angle ACE = 161°, what is the measure of Angle ECB?

4.MD.

2. If the hands on the clock show 3:00, how many degrees does the minute hand move until it is 3:45?

4.MD.7

5. The barn door turns 330° from open to close. If it is open 192°, how many degrees will it have to turn to be completely open?

4.MD.7

3. Angle K is 57 degrees. How many degrees is Angle J?

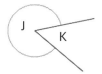

4.MD.7

6. What is the measurement of the angle below?

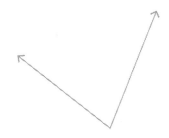

4.MD.6

1. Angle DAB is 121°. Angle CAD is 37°.

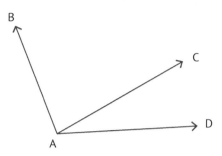

How many degrees is Angle CAB?

4.MD.7

4. If Angle R is 91 degrees, how many degrees is Angle T?

4.MD.7

Use the figure below to answer questions 2–3.

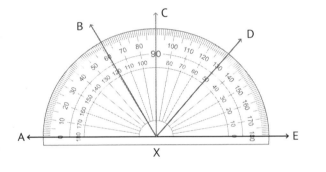

2. Angle CXA is 90° and Angle AXB is 61°. What is the measure of Angle CXB?

4.MD.7

3. Angle CXE is 90° and Angle DXE is 50°. What is the measure of Angle CXD?

4.MD.7

5. What is the closest measure for the angle below?

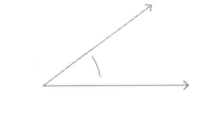

4.MD.6

6. If Angle ABC + Angle CBD = 210° and Angle ABC is 94°, what is the measure of Angle CBD?

4.MD.7

1. Using the figure below, Trey started at the top and then made a $\frac{1}{2}$ turn to the right. How many degrees did Trey turn?

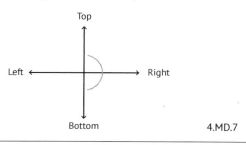

Top

Left

Right

Bottom

4.MD.7

4. Angle AXD is 180°. How many degrees i Angle BXC?

4.MD.

2. If Angle ABC + Angle CBE = 311° and Angle ABC is 254°, what is the measure of Angle CBE?

4.MD.7

5. The puppy weighs 10 pounds + 12 ounce and the cat weighs 9 pounds + 29 ounce: Which pet weighs the most? Show you work.

4.MD.2

Use the figure below to answer questions 3 – 4.

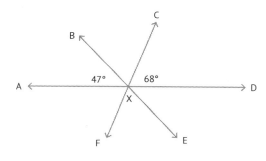

C

B

47°

68°

A

D

X

F

E

3. Angle BXE measures 180 degrees. If Angle FXE is 65 degrees, what is the measure of Angle FXA?

4.MD.7

6. If Angle J is 314 degrees. How man degrees is the Angle K?

J

K

4.MD.7

se the figure below to answer questions 1–3.

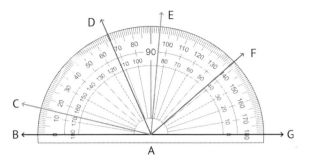

4. If Angle DEH is 180° and Angle AEH is 97°, what is the measure of Angle DEA?

4.MD.7

1. What is the measure of Angle EAC?

4.MD.7

5. If Angle HEF is 102° and Angle ZEH is 79°, what is Angle ZEF?

2. What is the measure of Angle FAD?

4.MD.7

4.MD.7

3. What is the measure of Angle EAD?

4.MD.7

se the figure below to answer questions 4–5.

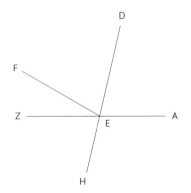

6. Lily had to unpack 38 boxes that each contained 19 backpacks. She then had to repack them so there were only 9 backpacks in a box. How many full boxes would Lily have and how many backpacks would be leftover? Show your work.

4.OA.3

1. What is the closest measure for the angle below?

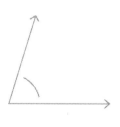

4.MD.6

3. If Angle FEG were 125°, and Angle GE were 152°, how many degrees woul Angle FEH be?

4.MD.

Use the figure below to answer questions 2–3.

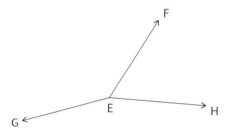

4. Chris swam the race in 98 seconds whil Sidney swam it in 1 minute, 35 second Who had the faster time? Show your worl

4.MD.2

2. If Angle HEG were 165° and Angle HEF were 79°, what would the measure of Angle GEF be?

4.MD.7

5. Angle T is 271 degrees. How man degrees is Angle R?

4.MD.7

DAY 6
CHALLENGE
QUESTION

Draw a large triangle. Measure each of its 3 angles. Add the angles together. What is their sum?

4.MD.7

WEEK 18

VIDEO EXPLANATIONS

ngles aren't the only geometry you'll be able to practice. This week you'll also have a chance to work with specific angles (right, acute, obtuse) and certain types of lines such as parallel and perpendicular lines.

You can find detailed video explanations to each problem in the book by visiting:
ArgoPrep.com

Use the shapes shown below to answer questions 1–3. Answers may have 0, 1 or more than 1 correct answer.

A   B   C   D   E   F

Use the figures shown below to answer questions 4–6. Answers may have 0, 1 or more than 1 correct answer.

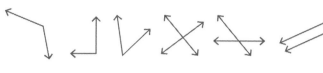

A   B   C   D   E   F

1. Which shape(s) contain at least 1 line segment?

4.G.1

4. Which figure(s) show perpendicular lines or rays?

4.G.

2. Which shape(s) has at least 1 right angle?

4.G.1

5. Which figure(s) show acute angles?

4.G.1

3. Which shape(s) have MORE than 1 angle that can be measured?

4.G.1

6. Which figure(s) show obtuse angles?

4.G.1

se the shapes shown below to answer
questions 1–5. Answers may have 0, 1 or more
an 1 correct answer.

A   B   C   D   E   F

1. Which shape(s) contain MORE than 3 pairs of parallel lines?

4.G.1

2. Which shape(s) have at least 1 right angle?

4.G.1

3. Which shape(s) are made of AT LEAST 3 line segments?

4.G.1

4. Which shape(s) contain EXACTLY 2 pairs of parallel lines?

4.G.1

5. Which shape(s) contain all acute angles?

4.G.1

6. Draw a shape that has 2 rays with a common endpoint and that measures as an acute angle.

4.G.1

Use the shapes shown below to answer questions 1–5. Answers may have 0, 1 or more than 1 correct answer.

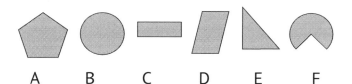

A   B   C   D   E   F

1. Which shape(s) have ZERO parallel lines?

4.G.1

2. Which shape(s) have at least 1 right angle?

4.G.1

3. Which shape(s) have AT LEAST 1 pair of perpendicular lines?

4.G.1

4. Which shape(s) contain AT LEAST 1 pair of parallel lines?

4.G.

5. Which shape(s) contain ZERO angles that can be measured?

4.G.1

6. A square has a perimeter of 28 m. What is the area of the square?

4.MD.3

ARGOPREP.COM

se the figures below to answer questions 1–5.
nswers may have 0, 1 or more than 1 correct
nswer.

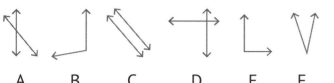

A   B   C   D   E   F

. Which figure(s) show parallel lines?

4.G.1

2. Which figure(s) show perpendicular lines?

4.G.1

3. Which figure(s) show acute angles?

4.G.1

4. Which figure(s) show obtuse angles?

4.G.1

5. Which figure(s) show rays?

4.G.1

6. To go on Sliding Rock, it takes 12 minutes waiting in line and then 2 minutes to ride down. If Tyler went on Sliding Rock 15 times, how much time did he spend waiting and riding?

4.MD.2

Use the figures below to answer questions 1–3. Answers may have 0, 1 or more than 1 correct answer.

Use the shapes shown below to answ questions 4–6. Answers may have 0, 1 or mo than 1 correct answer.

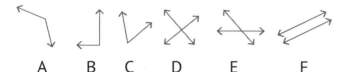

A   B   C   D   E   F

A   B   C   D   E   F

1. Which figure(s) show rays?

4.G.1

2. Which figure(s) show parallel lines?

4.G.1

3. Which figure(s) show right angles?

4.G.1

4. Which shape(s) have ALL acute angles?

4.G.

5. Which shape(s) have ONLY perpendicula or parallel lines?

4.G.

6. Which shape(s) contain AT LEAST obtuse angles?

4.G.

7. Using the data set below, how many mor units were $8\frac{1}{2}$ than were 8?

4.MD.

DAY 6
CHALLENGE
QUESTION

Draw a figure that has 4 sides, EXACTLY 1 pair of parallel lines and 2 right angles.

4.G.1

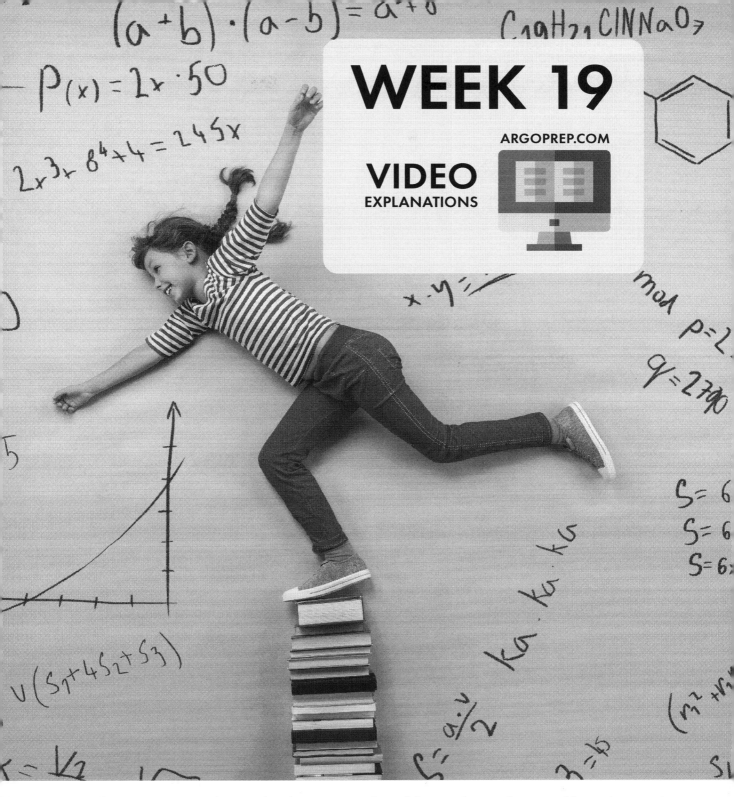

WEEK 19

This week you'll see geometric shapes that have examples of the angles and types of lines that you've worked with in the previous couple of weeks. You'll also find and draw right triangles.

You can find detailed video explanations to each problem in the book by visiting:
ArgoPrep.com

Use the figures below to answer questions 1 – 3. Use the figures below to answer questions 4 –

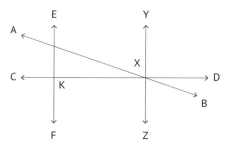

A   B   C   D   E   F

---

1. Name a right angle.

4.G.2

---

4. Which figure is a right triangle?

4.G.2

---

2. Which lines are parallel?

4.G.2

---

5. Which figure(s) have parallel lines?

4.G.2

---

3. Name a pair of perpendicular lines.

4.G.2

---

6. Which figure appears to have an angle that is 270 degrees?

4.MD.7

se the figures below to answer questions 1–4.

A   B   C   D   E   F

. Which figures do NOT have ANY parallel lines?

4.G.2

2. Which figure has EXACTLY 4 right angles?

4.G.2

3. Which figures have parallel lines?

4.G.2

4. Which figures appear to have ONLY obtuse angles?

4.G.2

5. Write a fraction that is equivalent to $\frac{4}{5}$.

4.NF.1

6. Angle N is 97°. What is the measure of Angle M?

4.MD.7

Use the figures below to answer questions 1–4.

A   B   C   D   E   F

1. Which figures have EXACTLY 2 pairs of parallel lines?

4.G.2

2. Which figures have AT LEAST 1 right angle?

4.G.2

3. Which figures have perpendicular lines?

4.G.2

4. Which figures have ZERO parallel lines?

4.G.2

5. What is the quotient when 5,321 i divided by 8?

4.NBT.6

6. Change these 2 numbers into standard form:

7 hundred thousands + 4 thousands + 5 tens + 8 ones **and**
7 × 100,000 + 4 × 1,000 + 5 × 100 + 8 tens

Write a comparison number sentence using the numbers in standard form.

4.NBT.2

1. Label the types of angles shown on each clock below.

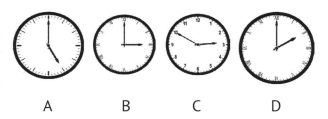

A   B   C   D

4.G.2

se the figures below to answer questions 2 – 5.

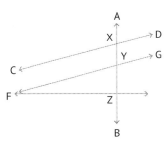

2. Which lines are parallel?

4.G.2

3. Name a right angle.

4.G.2

4. Which lines are perpendicular?

4.G.2

5. Name an obtuse angle.

4.G.2

6. What are the prime numbers between 40 and 50?

4.OA.4

Use the figures below to answer questions 1–4.

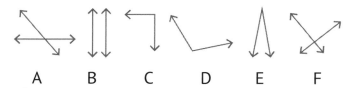

A   B   C   D   E   F

4. Which figures have acute angles?

4.G.

1. Which figures have right angles?

4.G.2

5. Write a multiplication sentence for the model below.

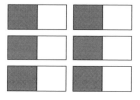

4.NF.

2. Which figures have obtuse angles?

4.G.2

3. Which figure has parallel lines?

4.G.2

6. How many degrees is an angle that is $\frac{1}{5}$ of a circle?

4.G.2

DAY 6
CHALLENGE
QUESTION

A. List 3 types of angles and describe them.
B. What is the difference between parallel and perpendicular lines?

4.MD.5

Using the geometric shapes from last week, we'll find lines of symmetry for them. Lines of symmetry are lines that perfectly divide a shape in half so that there are mirror images on either side of that line.

You can find detailed video explanations to each problem in the book by visiting:
ArgoPrep.com

WEEK 20 · DAY 1

Use the figures below to answer questions 1–2.

A   B   C   D   E   F

1. Which figures appear to have ZERO lines of symmetry?

4.G.3

2. Which figure appears to have EXACTLY 1 line of symmetry?

4.G.3

Use the figures below to answer questions 3–6.

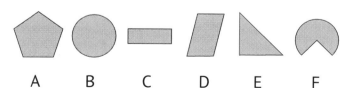

A   B   C   D   E   F

3. Which figures appear to have more tha 1 line of symmetry?

4.G.

4. Which figures have EXACTLY 1 line c symmetry?

4.G.

5. Which figures have ZERO lines c symmetry?

4.G.

6. Which figure is a right triangle?

4.G.2

e the letters below to answer questions 1–2.

A B C D E F

. Which letters have ZERO lines of symmetry?

4.G.3

. Which letters have EXACTLY 1 line of symmetry?

4.G.3

se the figures below to answer questions 3–5.

A   B   C   D   E   F

3. Which figures appear to have exactly 1 line of symmetry?

4.G.3

4. Which figures have AT LEAST 2 lines of symmetry?

4.G.3

5. Which figures have perpendicular lines?

4.G.2

1. Draw in the lines of symmetry for the figures below.

4.G.3

Use the figures below to answer questions 5-

A   B   C   D   E   F

Use the letters below to answer questions 2–4.

H P X T V R

2. Which letters have ZERO lines of symmetry?

4.G.3

5. Which figure does NOT appear to hav any line of symmetry?

4.G.3

3. Which letters have MORE than 1 line of symmetry?

4.G.3

6. How many lines of symmetry doe Figure C have?

4. Which letters have EXACTLY 1 line of symmetry?

4.G.3

4.G.3

se the letters below to answer questions 1–3. Use the figures below to answer questions 4–6.

M G Z U I K

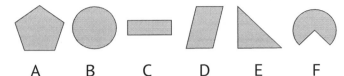

A   B   C   D   E   F

. Which letters have EXACTLY 1 line of symmetry?

4.G.3

---

4. Which figure appears to be a right triangle?

4.G.2

. Which letter has MORE than 1 line of symmetry?

4.G.3

---

5. Which figure has the most lines of symmetry?

4.G.3

. Which letters have ZERO lines of symmetry?

4.G.3

---

6. Which figures have EXACTLY 1 line of symmetry?

4.G.3

1. How many lines of symmetry does the figure below have?

4.G.3

2. What is $10 \frac{3}{5} + 18 \frac{4}{5}$?

4.NF.3

3. Which letters have 2 lines of symmetry?

4.G.

4. Which letters have ZERO lines of symmetry?

4.G.

5. Which letter has exactly 1 line of symmetry?

4.G.3

Use the letters below to answer questions 3–5.

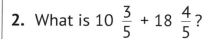

 N L J O W X

6. Draw in the lines of symmetry for the figures below.

4.G.3

 **DAY 6**
CHALLENGE
QUESTION

How many lines of symmetry does a circle have?

4.G.3

THE END!

Assessment

VIDEO EXPLANATIONS

ARGOPREP.COM

Great job finishing all 20 weeks! You should be ready for any test. Try this assessment to see how much you've learned - good luck!

1. Use the figure below to answer the question.

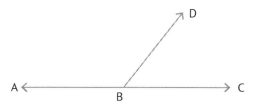

Angle ABC is 180° and Angle ABD is 123°, how many degrees is Angle DBC?

4.MD.

2. What do we know based on the equation 9 × 14 = 126?

4.OA.

3. The trail is 0.83 of a kilometer long. How long is the trail as a fraction?

4.NF.

4. Mason buys 4 pairs of tennis shoes, 12 pairs of socks and 2 pairs of sandals. What is the cost of Mason's purchase?

Type of Shoe	Price
Tennis	$158
Sandals	$39
Socks	$9

4.NBT.4

ARGOPREP.COM

5. Write these 2 numbers in standard form:
4 thousands + 6 hundreds + 2 ones
4 thousands + 7 ones + 3 hundreds
Now write a comparison number sentence using the 2 standard form numbers.

4.NBT.2

6. What is the missing number in the pattern? 97, 93, _____, 85

4.OA.5

7. Write the equation shown in the model below.

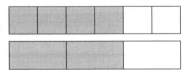

4.NF.1

8. List all of the factors for the following numbers:

A. 42
B. 43

4.OA.4

131

9. How many times greater is the 7 in 7,826 than the 7 in 735?

4.NBT.

10. What is $19\frac{1}{4} - 11\frac{3}{4}$?

4.NF.

11. The perimeter of the bedroom is 54 ft, if the length is 15 feet, what is the area?

4.MD.3

12. What is $\frac{5}{100} + \frac{2}{10}$?

4.NF.5

3. What is 46,197,588 rounded to the nearest ten thousand?

4.NBT.3

4. Which ordered pair would complete the table?

Feet	Inches
1	12
3	36

4.MD.1

5. Draw in the lines of symmetry for the following figures.

4.G.3

6. Miles had 12 cards and Jameson had 4. Write an equation that can be used to find how many *times* more cards Miles has.

4.OA.2

17. What is the quotient of 4562 and 9?

4.NBT.

18. There will be 35 people at the party. Each one will eat $\frac{2}{3}$ cup of yogurt.

   A. What equation can be used to find out how much yogurt, Y, will be eaten?
   B. How much yogurt will be eaten?

4.NF.

19. Write

   (a) an addition number sentence that is equivalent to $\frac{5}{3}$.
   (b) a multiplication number sentence that is equivalent to $\frac{5}{3}$.

4.NF.3
4.NF.4

20. Write a true number sentence using $\frac{1}{4}$ and $\frac{1}{3}$.

4.NF.2

21. What is the product of 5,832 and 7?

4.NBT.5

22. Michael ran 5 kilometers and Shawn ran 5000 meters. Who ran the farthest? Show your work.

4.MD.2

23. Krystal mowed $\frac{3}{8}$ of the lawn on Sunday and $\frac{2}{8}$ on Monday. How much of the lawn is left to mow?

4.NF.3

24. How many one-degree angles are in an angle that is 78°?

4.MD.5

25. Write an equation for the model below.

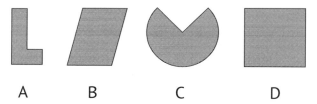

4.NF.

Use the figure below to answer the questions that follow.

A   B   C   D

26.A. Which of the figures have no parallel lines?
  B. Which of the figures have exactly ONE line of symmetry?

4.G.
4.G.

27. If an angle turns through $\frac{1}{2}$ of a circle, what is its measure?

4.MD.5

28. Use the data set below to answer the question that follows.

Height Increase (inches)

How many more students grew $\frac{1}{4}$ of an inch than those who grew $\frac{1}{2}$ an inch?

4.MD.4

29. Use the figures below to answer the questions that follow.

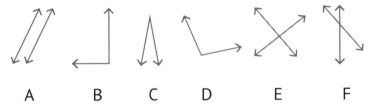

A   B   C   D   E   F

A. Which figures have acute angles?
B. Which figures have perpendicular angles?
C. Which figures have rays?

4.G.1

30. What is the sum of 792 and 1,048?

4.NBT.

31. Write a comparison number sentence using 1.4 and 1.39.

4.NF.

32. Use the figure below to answer the questions that follow.

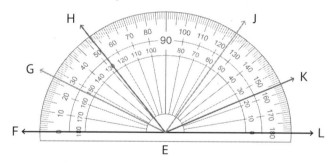

    A. What is the measure of Angle LEG?

    B. What is the measure of Angle HEJ?

4.MD.6
4.MD.7

33. Jeff wants to fence his yard. He knows it has an area of 450 square yards and is 15 yard wide. How much fencing would he need?

    A. 30 yards

    B. 90 yards

    C. 125 yards

    D. 465 yards

4.MD.3

4. What numbers are missing in the pattern below?

____, 37, 40, 43, ____, 49

A. 33 and 47
B. 33 and 46
C. 34 and 47
D. 34 and 46

4.OA.5

5. Which statement is true?

A. 13 < 12.98
B. 152.6 > 152.37
C. 431.49 = 431.5
D. 875.03 = 875.30

4.NF.7

36. Each cabin needs $\frac{3}{5}$ acre of land. If there are 12 cabins, how much land is needed?

A. $\frac{60}{3}$ acres

B. $12\frac{3}{5}$ acres

C. $\frac{36}{5}$ acres

D. $\frac{36}{60}$ acres

4.NF.4

37. Which number set contains ALL the factors of 24?

A. 1, 2, 4, 6, 8, 10, 12, 24
B. 1, 2, 3, 4, 6, 8, 12, 24
C. 1, 2, 3, 4, 8, 12, 24
D. 1, 2, 3, 6, 8, 12, 24

4.OA.4

38. What is six hundred thirty thousand, six hundred, twenty-nine in expanded form?

    A. (6 × 100,000) + (3 × 10,000) + (6 × 100) + (2 × 10) + (9 × 1)
    B. (6 × 100,000) + (3 × 1,000) + (6 × 100) + (2 × 10) + (9 × 1)
    C. (6 × 100,000) + (3 × 10,000) + (6 × 100) + (2 × 1) + (9 × 10)
    D. (6 × 100,000) + (3 × 1000) + (6 × 100) + (2 × 1) + (9 × 1)

4.NBT.

---

39. Which number sentence is modeled below?

    A. $\frac{4}{5} > \frac{9}{10}$ **B.** $\frac{9}{10} < \frac{4}{5}$

    C. $\frac{9}{10} = \frac{4}{5}$ **D.** $\frac{4}{5} < \frac{9}{10}$

4.NF.

---

40. Angle AXD is 180°. What is the measure of Angle AXB?

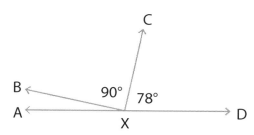

    A. 12°
    B. 22°
    C. 192°
    D. 258°

4.MD.7

41. Kenzi has 1 snake that is 3 feet and another snake that is 2 yards. Which number sentence is true?

   A. 3 feet > 2 yards
   B. 3 feet < 2 yards
   C. 2 yards < 3 feet
   D. 2 yards = 3 feet

4.MD.1

42. The chart below shows how many yards Tillie walked on some days. How many feet did she walk?

Day	Yards Walked
Monday	971
Wednesday	805
Friday	698

   A. 825
   B. 2,474
   C. 5,328
   D. 7,422

4.MD.2

43. Carlisle had $5,960 saved for college and Jessa had $5,690 saved. Which statement is true?

   A. Carlisle had more because 5960 > 5690.
   B. Carlisle had more because 5960 < 5690.
   C. Jessa had more because 5960 > 5690.
   D. Jessa had more because 5960 < 5690.

4.NBT.2

ANSWER KEYS

VIDEO EXPLANATIONS

ARGOPREP.COM

ANSWER KEYS

WEEK 1

DAY 1
1. 70 miles
2. 7 bills
3. 40 boxes
4. 500
5. 6 miles
6. 100

DAY 2
1. 30 minutes
2. 4 years old
3. 8
4. $10
5. 10
6. 100 meters

DAY 3
1. 48,216
2. Sixteen thousand, four hundred twelve
3. 57,819 < 58,016 or 58,016 > 57,819
4. 589,002
5. 14,982 < 41,237 or 41,237 > 14,982
6. Any number between 400 – 499 will work.

DAY 4
1. 12,457 > 12,398 or 12,398 < 12,457
2. 608,571
3. 175,403
4. One hundred twenty-five thousand, eighty-one
5. 7,863
6. 700,000 + 50,000 + 2 + 10 = 750,012

DAY 5
1. 20,000
2. Two hundred fifty-four thousand, ninety-two
3. 27,435
4. 300 acres
5. 6,045 < 6,405 or 6,405 > 6,045
6. 50

WEEK 2

Day 1
1. 1,690 and 1,700
2. 13,697,050 < 13,700,000 or 13,700,000 > 13,697,0503.
3. 15,000
4. 68,000
5. 349,800 < 350,000 or 350,000 > 349,800
6. 7,000

Day 2
1. 76,000,000 and 76,050,000
2. 79,100,000
3. If 672 were rounded to the hundreds place it would be 700. If 672 were rounded to the tens place, it would be 670.
4. 981,700 and 980,000
5. 8,800,000
6. 150

Day 3
1. 327
2. $6806
3. 9,000 – 4,000 = 5,000
4. 4,671 – 3,640 = 1,031 or 4,671 – 1,031 = 3,640 or 1,031 + 3,640 = 4,671
5. 8,105

Day 4
1. 2,600 + 3,800 = 6,400
2. 4,603
3. 8,315
4. 385
5. 5,680; 2,871

Day 5
1. Any number from 8,050 – 8,149
2. 7,890 – 4,530 = 3,360
3. 9,000,000 and 8,529,000
4. $2,470
5. 4,615
6. 5,600 < 5,800 or 5,800 > 5,600

WEEK 3

Day 1
1. 3,192
2. 1,828
3. 768
4. 330, 248, 578, 990

Day 2
1. 6,340
2. 18,292
3. 5,000
4. 18,400
5. 11,682

Day 3
1. 333 bunches with 3 leftover
2. 85 boxes; There will be 2 pairs left unpacked because 512 divided by 6 is 85 remainder 2.
3. 38 trips; 5 chairs
4. 3,893
5. 3,009 loveseats

Day 4
1. The boxes that hold 8 will have no leftover cupcakes because $\frac{3200}{6} = 533$ r 2 and $\frac{3200}{8} = 400$ r 0.
2. 27 tables, 4 people
3. 48 trays
4. 20 trays, 2 leftover
5. 15 trays, 11 trays

Day 5
1. A. 2,205 B. 276 C. 5
2. 11,025
3. 11,000
4. 2,832 gallons
5. 328 gallons

WEEK 4

Day 1
1. 42 = 14 × 3 or similar
2. 4, 2, 6
3. 3 times
4. 2 times
5. 542,000 = 542,000

Day 2
1. The number 12 is 4 times larger than the number 3. (The 3 and the 4 could be switched and the statement would still be correct.) The number 12 is 6 times larger than the number 2. (The 6 and the 2 could be switched and the statement would still be correct.)
2. 28 = 4 × 7 or similar
3. 28 parachutes, 8 left
4. The number 30 is 6 times as large as the number 5. The number 30 is 5 times as large as the number 6.
5. 4 times as old as Ralphie, 2 times as old as Ralphie
6. 72 = 8 × 9 or similar

Day 3
1. The model can look something like this:

20			
5	5	5	5

2. A. 378 B. 504
3. A. 6 B. 36
4. 3 times, 2 times
5. A. 49 B. 56

Day 4
1. 8 hours
2. 24 days, 32 days
3. 3 × 5 = 15 or 5 × 3 = 15
4. 2 weeks; 14 weeks
5. 128 minutes; 160 minutes

Day 5
1. A. 3,705 B. 96
2. 718 miles
3. $325, $390
4. 5
5. 16 inches, 24 inches

WEEK 5

Day 1
1. 9,937
2. 1,419
3. 4
4. 3,640 > 3,604 or 3,604 < 3,640
5. M = 596 × 8
   B. $4768

Day 2
1. 1,550 cushions, 387 boxes, 2 cushions
2. A. 7,962 B. 3,981 C. 0
3. 1,176
4. 7,900 > 7,890 or 7,890 < 7,905
5. $R = \frac{2350 + 316 + 298}{6}$; $494

Day 3
1. 10, 20, 30, 40, 50
2. 18: 1, 2, 3, 6, 9, 18; 24: 1, 2, 3, 4, 6, 8, 12, 24; 24 has more factors (8 > 6)
3. 24, 48, 72, 96
4. 12: 1, 2, 3, 4, 6, 12, 15: 1, 3, 5, 15. 12 has more factors (6 > 4)
5. $1,672
6. Because 6 is a multiple of 2 and 3 (6 = 2 × 3), all numbers that are multiples of 2 AND 3, will also be multiples of 6.

Day 4
1. 6, 12, 18, 24, 30
2. 32 = 1, 2, 4, 8, 16, 32; 36 = 1, 2, 3, 6, 12, 18, 36; 36 has more factors (9 > 6)
3. Because 9 is a multiple of 3 (9 = 3 × 3), all numbers that are multiples of 9, will also be multiples of 3.
4. The belts could be packaged in packages of 2, 3, 4, 6, 8 or 12.
5. $C = \frac{9860}{6}$
   1,643 cartons, 2 eggs
6. 15: 1, 3, 5, 15; 21: 1, 3, 7, 21; They have the same number of factors (4 = 4)

Day 5
1. The water could be packaged in bottles of 2, 3, 6, or 9 bottles.
2. 55 miles; 11 miles
3. $405
4. 10: 1, 2, 5, 10; 14: 1, 2, 7, 14; 18: 1, 2, 3, 6, 9, 18; 18 has more factors (6 > 4)
5. Because 10 is a multiple of 2 and 5 (10 = 2 × 5), all numbers that are multiples of 2 AND 5, will also be multiples of 10.

WEEK 6

Day 1
1. Answers should begin with an even number and then add 5 to every number after that. Two examples are 4, 9, 14, 19 or 10, 15, 20, 25.
2. Emma; Add 3: 12, 15, 18, 21, 24, 27, 30; Add 5: 10, 14, 18, 22, 26, 30
3. 47, 44, 41, 38
4. 24 has more factor pairs because 4 pairs > 3 pairs; 99: 1, 33, 9, 11, 3, 33; 24: 1, 24, 2, 12, 8, 4, 6
5. Any answer where the shapes have 2 less each time follow the rule. One example is given below.

6. Subtract 10

Day 2
1. Subtract 2; Any shape that has 6 circles is fine.; One example:

2. Tom; Subtract 5: 42, 37, 32, 27, 22, 17, 12; Subtract 2: 22, 20, 18, 16, 14, 12
3. 29, 35, 41, 47
4. 4,090 = 4,090
5. Caroline; Add 3: 0, 3, 6, 9, 12, 15, 18, 21; Add 2: 9, 11, 13, 15, 17, 19, 21

Day 3
1. Answers may look similar to these:

2. $\frac{2}{3} = \frac{4}{6}$
3. $\frac{3}{5}$
4. Answers may look similar to these:

5. $316; $35; $281

Day 4
1. Answers may look similar to these:

2. $\frac{4}{10} = \frac{2}{5}$
3. Answers may look similar to these:

4. Answers may include: $\frac{1}{3}, \frac{2}{6}, \frac{3}{9}$ or $\frac{5}{15}$
5. Any number that has the 5's next to each other is correct. A couple of examples are 5,541 or 4,155 or 1,554.

Day 5
1. $\frac{4}{5} = \frac{8}{10}$
2. Suitable answers include: $\frac{1}{2}, \frac{4}{8}, \frac{3}{6}, \frac{5}{10}$
3. 47, 43, 39, 35
4. Add 4
5. Boris; Subtract 4: 100, 96, 92, 88, 84, 80, 76, 72; Subtract 3: 90, 87, 84, 81, 78, 75, 72

WEEK 7

Day 1
1. $\frac{1}{2} < \frac{5}{8}$ and $\frac{5}{8} > \frac{1}{2}$
2. Dino; Rex
3. Answer may look something like this:

4. Answer may look something like this:

5. Brody; Austin

Day 2
1. Answers may look something like this:

2. 15; $\frac{6}{15}$ and $\frac{5}{15}$; $\frac{2}{5} > \frac{1}{3}$
3. $\frac{1}{2} < \frac{2}{3}$ and $\frac{2}{3} > \frac{1}{2}$
4. $\frac{5}{6} > \frac{3}{4}$ and $\frac{3}{4} < \frac{5}{6}$
5. 10 miles

Day 3
1. $\frac{1}{2} < \frac{5}{8}$ or $\frac{5}{8} > \frac{1}{2}$
2. Answer may look something like this:

3. A; B
4. 12; $\frac{7}{12}$ and $\frac{9}{12}$; $\frac{7}{12} < \frac{3}{4}$
5. E = 4 × B

Day 4
1. $\frac{2}{3} < \frac{3}{4}$ and $\frac{3}{4} > \frac{2}{3}$
2. 22; $\frac{11}{22}$ and $\frac{10}{22}$; $\frac{1}{2} > \frac{5}{11}$
3. Michelle; Amanda
4. $2,987
5. 24; $\frac{9}{24}$ and $\frac{10}{24}$; $\frac{3}{8} < \frac{5}{12}$

Day 5
1. $\frac{6}{15} > \frac{1}{3}$ and $\frac{1}{3} < \frac{6}{15}$
2. $\frac{4}{5} < \frac{5}{6}$ and $\frac{5}{6} > \frac{4}{5}$
3. Answers may look something like this:

4. 1, 2, 3, and 6
5. 18; $\frac{15}{18}$ and $\frac{16}{18}$; $\frac{5}{6} < \frac{8}{9}$

WEEK 8

Day 1
1. $\frac{8}{3}$; $\frac{4}{3}$
2. $3\frac{6}{8}$
3. $8\frac{3}{4}$ hours
4. 5 vans; 8 students
5. $\frac{28}{5}$ miles or $5\frac{3}{5}$ miles
6. $\frac{1}{7} + \frac{1}{7} + \frac{1}{7} + \frac{1}{7} = \frac{4}{7}$

Day 2
1. $5\frac{7}{9}$ gallons; 34 gallons; $3\frac{5}{9}$ gallons
2. $9\frac{2}{3}$ miles
3. 79, 75, 71, 67
4. $\frac{1}{5} + \frac{1}{5} + \frac{1}{5} = \frac{3}{5}$
5. $\frac{6}{8}$ feet

Day 3
1. $2\frac{1}{4}$; $27\frac{3}{4}$
2. $\frac{10}{4}$ CUPS; $\frac{7}{4}$ CUPS
3. $\frac{80}{5}$ or 16 gallons
4. $\frac{1}{6} + \frac{1}{6} = \frac{2}{6}$
5. $15,000 and $14,970

Day 4
1. 6 hours
2. Answers may look similar to this example:

3. $1 + 1 + \frac{1}{5} + \frac{1}{5} = 2\frac{2}{5}$
4. Answers may include: $\frac{1}{3}, \frac{2}{6}, \frac{3}{9}$ or $\frac{5}{15}$
5. 228

Day 5
1. $\frac{24}{5}$ or $4\frac{4}{5}$ POUNDS
2. Answers may look like this model:

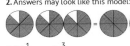

3. $37\frac{1}{4}$ cups; $5\frac{3}{4}$ cups
4. 10
5. $1 + 1 + 1 + \frac{1}{3} + \frac{1}{3} = 3\frac{2}{3}$

WEEK 9

Day 1
1. $\frac{9}{4}$
2. $\frac{35}{6}$ GAL
3. $5 × \frac{4}{15} = \frac{20}{15}$
4. $\frac{4}{15} + \frac{4}{15} + \frac{4}{15} + \frac{4}{15} + \frac{4}{15} = \frac{20}{15}$
5. $\frac{14}{3}$ IN

Day 2
1. $\frac{16}{3}$ yards
2. $\frac{9}{4}$
3. $4 × \frac{1}{2} = \frac{4}{2}$
4. $1\frac{1}{5}$ granola bars
5. $\frac{32}{7}$ acres

Day 3
1. $\frac{2}{5} × 3 = \frac{6}{5}$
2. $\frac{63}{8}$ kg
3. $\frac{7}{2}$ pounds
4. $\frac{32}{5}$ KM
5. 4 glasses

Day 4
1. $\frac{15}{4}$ hour
2. $\frac{45}{10}$ MIN
3. $\frac{9}{8}$ CUP
4. $\frac{6}{10} = \frac{3}{5}$
5. $\frac{5}{3}$ cans

Day 5
1. $\frac{18}{5}$ hours
2. $\frac{15}{2}$ cups
3. $\frac{5}{4}$ hours
4. $\frac{3}{4} < \frac{7}{8}$ and $\frac{7}{8} > \frac{3}{4}$
5. $4 × \frac{1}{5} = \frac{4}{5}$

WEEK 10

Day 1
1. $\frac{47}{100}$ of a dollar
2. $\frac{5}{10}$ and $\frac{10}{10}$; $\frac{50}{100}$ and $\frac{10}{100}$
3. $\frac{60}{100}$ or $\frac{6}{10}$
4. $\frac{73}{100}$
5. A. 9,008 B. 2,552

Day 2
1. $\frac{44}{100}$ inches
2. $\frac{52}{100}$ of an hour
3. $\frac{39}{100}$ of a yard
4. $\frac{1}{7} + \frac{1}{7} + \frac{1}{7} + \frac{1}{7} = \frac{4}{7}$; $4 × \frac{1}{7} = \frac{4}{7}$
5. $\frac{83}{100}$ of a foot

Day 3
1. $\frac{39}{100}$ of an inch
2. 0.57 and 0.4
3. $\frac{50}{100} = \frac{5}{10}$ OR 0.50 = 0.5
4. 0.6
5. 0.13

Day 4
1. 0.8
2. 0.46
3. $2 × \frac{1}{3} = \frac{2}{3}$
4. 0.89
5. 0.33

Day 5
1. 0.06
2. $\frac{41}{100}$ of a mile
3. $\frac{90}{100}$ or $\frac{9}{10}$ of a yard
4. 0.51
5. D
6. A

ANSWER KEYS

WEEK 11

Day 1
1. 0.3 > 0.27 or 0.27 < 0.3
2. 0.80 = 0.8
3. 0.09 < 0.9 or 0.9 > 0.09
4. 117,500 and 100,000
5. Day 2, Day 1, Day 3

Day 2
1. 0.94 < 0.98 or 0.98 > 0.94
2. Coin C, Coin B, Coin A
3. 15: 1, 3, 5, 15; 25: 1, 5, 25; 15 has more factors (4 > 3)
4. 0.45 > 0.4 or 0.4 < 0.45
5. 0.8 > 0.74 or 0.74 < 0.8

Day 3
1. 0.1 > 0.01 or 0.01 < 0.1
2. 0.42 < 0.5 or 0.5 > 0.42
3. Lookout, Overland, Dutch Pass
4. $1225
5. 0.29 < 0.3 or 0.3 > 0.29

Day 4
1. 0.39 < 0.7 or 0.7 > 0.39
2. 0.2 < 0.58 or 0.58 > 0.2
3. 0.53 > 0.5 or 0.5 < 0.53
4. 9, 18, 27 and 36
5. 0.6 > 0.49 or 0.49 < 0.6

Day 5
1. 0.32 > 0.3 or 0.3 < 0.32
2. belt, hat, socks
3. 0.66 < 0.7 or 0.7 > 0.66
4. 0.71 > 0.07 or 0.07 < 0.71
5. $\frac{6}{8}$ of a pound

WEEK 12

Day 1
1. 5,280 yards; 15,840 feet
2. (2, 200)
3. 5,000 meters; 5 times
4. F = 100 × 3; 300 feet
5. Any answers where the shapes have 3 less each time follow the rule. One example is given below.

Day 2
1. Because there are 12 inches in 1 foot, 1 foot is 12 times longer than 1 inch.
2. 4500 cm
3. (20, 200)
4. W = 4 × 16; 64 ounces
5. 2091 × 3 = 6273 and 75 × 84 = 6300 so 75 × 84 produces a larger number.

Day 3
1. (2, 120)
2. 97,000 meters
3. 9,000 grams
4. 240 seconds
5. (36)

Day 4
1. R = 16 × 3; 48 feet
2. 96 hours
3. 7 meters = 700 cm so Luke jumped farther because 700 > 698
4. 6,000 milliliters
5. $\frac{16}{3}$ miles
6. 72 inches

Day 5
1. (2, 6)
2. C = 2 × 1000; 2,000 grams
3. 80 ounces
4. 1000 times
5. 120 minutes

WEEK 13

Day 1
1. The garage door was 8 feet or 96 inches (8 × 12 = 96). The house door was also 96 inches or 8 feet ($\frac{96}{12}$ = 8). Both doors were the same height.
2. 9 hours, 45 minutes
3. 3,000
4. 3 feet = 36 inches. 36 > 33 so Nathan is taller.
5. 5 hours = 300 minutes. Mr. Evans cooked the turkey longer because 300 > 270.
6. 3 km = 3000 m. 3000 + 1,106 = 4,106 m

Day 2
1. 380 minutes; 20 minutes
2. 25 cm = 250 mm. The blue marker was longer because 250 < 260.
3. 12 hours
4. beef; 8 ounces
5. 3 hours = 180 minutes. Caleb talked longer because 180 > 175.
6. 7,450

Day 3
1. 32 meters
2. 13 yards; 42 yards
3. 58 feet
4. 264 feet²
5. F = 13 × $\frac{1}{8}$; $\frac{13}{8}$ cups
6. 15 feet; 225 ft2

Day 4
1. 17 feet; 238 ft2
2. 16 meters; 50 meters
3. 234 square inches
4. 12 feet; 120 ft²
5. 15 cm; 44 cm
6. 56: 1, 2, 4, 7, 8, 14, 28, 56; 99: 1, 3, 9, 11, 33, 99; The number 56 has more factors (8 > 6).

Day 5
1. Ruth drank more, 810 + 1300 = 2100 mL; 2L = 2000 mL and 2110 > 2000.
2. Length = 24 feet; Area = 240 square feet
3. 36 feet
4. 10 hours
5. 10/24 or 5/12

WEEK 14

Day 1
1. Answer:

2. 10 days
3. $\frac{3}{4}$ inch; 0 inches
4. 1 more day
5. $\frac{4}{10}$ and $\frac{8}{10}$; 0.4 and 0.8
6. 32 centimeters

Day 2
1. 15
2. $\frac{7}{8}$ of a gallon
3. 21 $\frac{7}{8}$ gallons
4. 2 $\frac{3}{4}$ pounds
5. 3 students
6. 7 students

Day 3
1. 12 × 6 = 72
2. hours; 20 students
3. 9 hours
4. 11 students
5. 3 students
6. 1, 45, 3, 15, 5, 9

Day 4
1. 5 cups
2. 4
3. $\frac{1}{4}$ cup
4. 40 bands
5. Answers may look something like this:

Day 5
1. 21
2. 8 $\frac{3}{4}$
3. 2
4. 7 $\frac{3}{4}$
5. 4

WEEK 15

Day 1
1. 77°
2. 90°, 180°, 36°
3. 60°
4. Answer may look something like this:

5. 321°

Day 2
1. 275°
2. 98 miles
3. 30°
4. 45°
5. 103°
6. 90°

Day 3
1. 180°
2. 120°, 60°, 30°
3. $\frac{86}{100}$
4. 90°
5. 117°

Day 4
1. 72°
2. 45°
3. 135°
4. 64 inches
5. 90°
6. P = $\frac{3}{5}$ × 11; $\frac{33}{5}$ pounds or 6 $\frac{3}{5}$ pounds

Day 5
1. 90°
2. 259
3. 36°
4. 1 and 3
5. 72°
6. 90°

WEEK 16

Day 1
1. Angle J = 30°, Angle K = 60°. Answers may vary slightly but the 2 numbers should equal 90 when added.
2. Both Angles A and B = 60°.
3. 61; 50
4. 1,336406
5. 90°
6. Subtract 3; 56

Day 2
1. 124 degrees; 180 degrees
2. 53; 24
3. 45
4. Answers should look something like this:

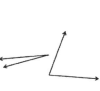

5. Angle C = 108°, Angle D = 72°. Answers may vary slightly but the 2 numbers should equal 180 when added.
6. 10 times

Day 3
1. 112 degrees; 14 degrees
2. 112; 137
3. $20,000 b. $18,300
4. Angle G = 40°, Angle H = 75°. Answers may vary slightly but should be close.
5. Answers should looks similar to this:

E ———————————————— F

Day 4
1. 39
2. 61
3. 180
4. 72 degrees
5. Angle U = 19°, Angle K = 71°. Answers may vary slightly but the 2 numbers should equal 90 when added.
6. $\frac{1}{4} \times 7 = \frac{7}{4}$ and $\frac{1}{4} + \frac{1}{4} + \frac{1}{4} + \frac{1}{4} + \frac{1}{4} + \frac{1}{4} + \frac{1}{4} = 7/4$

Day 5
1. 44 degrees
2. 50 degrees
3. 129
4. 180
5. 0.7 > 0.53
6. Answers will vary but should look something like this:

H

WEEK 17

Day 1
1. 84°
2. 270°
3. 303°
4. 124°
5. 138°
6. 68°

Day 2
1. 84°
2. 29°
3. 40°
4. 269°
5. 43°
6. 116°

Day 3
1. 180°
2. 57°
3. 68°
4. 65
5. 10 lbs + 12 oz = 172 oz; 9 lbs + 29 oz = 173 oz; 173 > 172 so the cat weighs more.
6. 46°

Day 4
1. 81°
2. 70°
3. 27°
4. 83°
5. 23°
6. 80 boxes &2 backpacks left

Day 5
1. 75°
2. 116°
3. 83°
4. 1 minute + 35 seconds = 9
5. 95 < 98 seconds so Sidney's time was faster.
6. 89°

WEEK 18

Day 1
1. A, B, D, E
2. A, D
3. B, D, E
4. B, D
5. C, E
6. A, E

Day 2
1. None
2. A, D, F
3. A, B, C, D, E, F
4. D, F
5. C
6. Any answer that has an angle that measures less than 90 degrees is correct. Correct drawings may look like this:

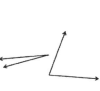

Day 3
1. A, B, E, F
2. C, E, F
3. C, E, F
4. C, D
5. B
6. 49 m²

Day 4
1. C
2. D, E
3. A, F
4. A, B
5. B, E, F
6. 210 minutes or 3 hours + 30 minutes

Day 5
1. A, B, C
2. F
3. B, D
4. F
5. A, D
6. B, C
7. 2

WEEK 19

Day 1
1. EKD, EKC, CKF, DKF, YXD, ZXC, YXC, or DXZ
2. EF and YZ
3. EF and CD or CD and YZ
4. A
5. C and D
6. E

Day 2
1. B and D
2. C
3. A, C, E and F
4. D and F
5. Answers may vary but some examples are $\frac{8}{10}$, 12/15, 20/25
6. 263°

Day 3
1. B and F
2. A, D, E, F
3. A, D, E, F
4. C and D
5. 665 r 1
6. 704,058 < 704,580

Day 4
1. **A** – obtuse, **B** – right, **C** – obtuse, **D** – acute
2. DC and FG
3. Any angle that has Z as the vertex is correct.
4. AB and FZ
5. CXA, BXD, AYF, or BYG
6. 41, 43, 47

Day 5
1. C and F
2. A and D
3. B
4. A and E
5. $\frac{1}{2} \times 6 = \frac{6}{2}$
6. 72°

WEEK 20

Day 1
1. A, B, D, E
2. C
3. A, B, C
4. F
5. D, E
6. E

Day 2
1. F
2. A, B, C, D, E
3. B, D, E
4. A, C, F
5. A. D

Day 3
1. Answer:

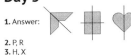

2. P, R
3. H, X
4. T, V
5. A
6. 8

Day 4
1. M, U
2. I
3. G, Z, K
4. E
5. B
6. A, F

Day 5
1. 4
2. 29 $\frac{2}{5}$
3. O, X
4. N, L, J
5. W
6. Answer:

ANSWER KEYS

CHALLENGE QUESTIONS

Week 1
97,540

Week 2
8,499

Week 3
11 times Asheboro's mammals because 11 × 98 = 1,078 and 9 × 108 = 972.
117 reptiles

Week 4
Marty had 30 points and Paul had 2 points.

Week 5
2 shells $14 each
4 shells for $7 each
7 shells for $4 each
14 shells for $2 each

Week 6
Kammi
Add 5: 9, 14, 19, 24
Add 1: 20, 21, 22, 23, 24
Add 3: 12, 15, 18, 21, 24

Week 7
Answer may look something like this:

▨▨ ☐ ☐	1/3
▨▨ ☐ ☐ ☐	2/5
▨▨▨▨▨▨▨ ☐☐☐☐☐☐☐☐	7/15

Week 8
$66 \frac{4}{5}$ pounds

Week 9
Robert;
Robert ran $\frac{4}{5}$ miles more.

Week 10
0.47 of an inch

Week 11
0.07, 0.3, 0.44

Week 12
1km = 1000m so 8km = 8000m;
1m = 100 cm so 8000m = 800,000cm

Week 13
Area is 153 m²
Perimeter is 52m

Week 14
A. Subtract 11
B. 66

Week 15
Because Angle A is 1/3 of a circle, it is 120°. Angle B turns through 186 one-degree angles so it is 186°. Angle C is the inside angle of a square which is a right angle so it is is 90°.
From smallest to largest, the angles are C, A, B.

Week 16
Angle AXB + Angle BXC = 90 degrees and Angle CXD + Angle DXE = 90 degrees.

Week 17
The angles in a triangle add up to 180 degrees.

Week 18
Students should have drawn a trapezoid that contains a right angle. Figures may vary but they might look like this:

Week 19
Acute angles are < 90°. Obtuse angles are > 90° Right angles are exactly 90°. Parallel lines never intersect and perpendicular lines intersect to form right angles.

Week 20
Circles have an unlimited number of lines of symmetry.

1. 57°

2. 126 is 14 times larger than 9 and 126 is 9 times larger than 14

3. $\frac{83}{100}$

4. $818

5. 4,602 > 4,307

6. 89

7. $\frac{4}{6} = \frac{2}{3}$

8. A. 1, 2, 3, 6, 7, 14, 21, 42; **B.** 1, 43

9. 10 times

10. $7\frac{2}{4}$

11. 180 ft²

12. $\frac{25}{100}$

13. 46,200,000

14. (2, 24)

15. Answer:

16. 4 × 3 = 12

17. 506 r 8

18. $35 \times \frac{2}{3} = ?$; $\frac{70}{3}$ cups

19. $\frac{1}{3} + \frac{1}{3} + \frac{1}{3} + \frac{1}{3} + \frac{1}{3} = \frac{5}{3}$; $5 \times \frac{1}{3} = \frac{5}{3}$

20. $\frac{1}{4} < \frac{1}{3}$ or $\frac{1}{3} > \frac{1}{4}$

21. 40,824

22. They ran the same distance because 5 km = 5000 m.

23. 3/8

24. 78

25. $4 \times \frac{1}{3} = \frac{4}{3}$

26. C; C

27. 180°

28. 5

29. A. C, F
   B. B, E
   C. B, C, D

30. 1,840

31. 1.4 > 1.39

32. 153°; 71°

33. B.

34. D.

35. B.

36. C.

37. B.

38. A.

39. B.

40. A.

41. B.

42. D.

43. A.

81661929R00084

Made in the USA
Middletown, DE
26 July 2018